Cookie Swap

COOKIE SWAP

Creative Treats to Share Throughout the Year

Julia M. Usher

Photographs by Steve Adams

GIBBS SMITH

TO ENRICH AND INSPIRE HUMANKIND

Salt Lake City | Charleston | Santa Fe | Santa Barbara

In memory of my sweet Dad.

The only thing bigger than his appetite for learning
was his unconditional support. Dad, I miss you.

First Edition
13 12 11 10 09   5 4 3 2 1

Text © 2009 Julia M. Usher
Photographs © 2009 Steve Adams

Published by
Gibbs Smith
P.O. Box 667
Layton, Utah 84041
Orders: 1.800.835.4993
www.gibbs-smith.com
Designed by Jocelyn Foye
Printed and bound in China
Gibbs Smith books are printed on either recycled, 100% post-consumer waste, FSC-certified
papers or on paper produced from a 100% certified sustainable forest/controlled wood source.

Library of Congress Cataloging-in-Publication Data

Usher, Julia M.
  Cookie swap : creative treats to share throughout the year / Julia M. Usher ; photographs by
Steve Adams. — 1st ed.
     p. cm.
  Includes index.
  ISBN-13: 978-1-4236-0378-8
  ISBN-10: 1-4236-0378-8
  1. Cookies. 2. Entertaining. I. Title.
  TX772.U75 2009
  641.8'654—dc22
                    2008054224

CONTENTS

ACKNOWLEDGMENTS

As much as the day-to-day act of writing is a solitary occupation, the four-year making of this book was truly a collaborative effort. Many thanks to my agent Sorche Fairbank; the talented team at Gibbs Smith, including Suzanne Taylor, Lisa Anderson, Jocelyn Foye, and Jennifer King; photographer-extraordinaire and good friend Steve Adams for keeping me ever mindful of the big picture; Elizabeth Maxson and Susan Jackson for their contributions to the book proposal; and Diann Cage for the wildly clever save-the-date and invitation designs that appear in the garden party chapter.

My gratitude also goes out to my cadre of recipe testers from the Saint Louis Culinary Society—Jamie Bommarito, Barbara Franck, Shirley Frost, Sandy Hounsom, Lynn Krause, Tana Lewis, Phyllis Meagher, Maria Sakellariou, Cari Schaeffer, Gail Streepy, and Mary Sutkus—and to Joy Bogen, Denise Dickey, Nicole Hanse, Georgeanne Keirstead, and Betsy Usher-Gmerek, a group of exceptionally capable moms who provided valuable feedback on the book's projects and games for kids.

Without the generosity, trust, and very lovely props and venues donated by so many people, I would never have been able to pull off this project. Thank you to the owners of The White Rabbit, Roots, Quintessential Antiques, Now and Then Antiques and Collectibles, Hammond's Books, Jon Paul Designs and Collectibles, Gringo Jones, Reed-Donovan Galleries, Sagaform, and Panorama. Also, thank you to Nancy Zitzmann, Tim Brown, and the fourth-grade class at Bristol School; Don Furjes and the staff at Avery School; the third-grade students at Holy Redeemer Catholic School; Kevin O'Neill at the historic Chatillon-DeMenil Mansion; Linda Pilcher; and Frances Gay for the use of her enviable garden. Special appreciation goes to Carol Fyhrie, Chris Priest, and the staff and dealers at Warson Woods Antique Gallery for the wealth of props donated for every chapter.

Perhaps it goes without saying, but I'll say it anyway: I am profoundly indebted to my parents—Mom for taking me under her wing in the kitchen and for showing me the joy of baking from scratch at a very early age, and Dad for always being there for me. Even in the late stages of Alzheimer's, he never forgot to ask how my writing was going.

Lastly, all my love to Bryan. In addition to being the world's most patient husband, he's proved over the course of this project to be a skilled taster, editor, publicist, and therapist too.

INTRODUCTION

I've had a long love affair with cookie swaps. From what my mother tells me, my infatuation began in 1965. I was a young child, and the scene was my father's company Christmas party on a snowy New England eve.

From the very start, the hot pink daisy-shaped spritz cookies called out to me. Their color was captivating, and their form—so wondrously regular, so pretty and polished—was completely uncharacteristic of the gingersnaps and chocolate-nut wafers that Mom always made. Better yet, they were sitting at the edge of the table, well within my reach. Not sure how long the coast would stay clear, I lunged toward the daisies and began a rapid cycling of hand to mouth. A few minutes later, I was in heaven, telltale pink crumbs clinging to my ear-to-ear grin.

Somewhere around my fifth or sixth fistful, my dad approached me with a plastic-wrapped plate of daisies, patted my now rumbling tummy, and told me not to worry. "Honey," he assured me, "at this party, you're expected to take home what you can't eat here." A great sense of relief came over me as I digested the significance of what he said. Not only did this party boast cookies never before seen in my house, but the trading of them meant I could savor them as long as I wanted without any rush. Amazing cookies. No empty stomachs. Plenty for all to divvy up and enjoy. This party was clearly special in so many ways.

Forty-plus years have since passed, and to this day, the pink daisy-shaped spritz cookie remains one of my cookie-swap favorites. By baking and sharing it with others, I keep the memory of my first cookie swap exactly where I want it—close to my heart. (You'll find the recipe for Pink Spritz Daisy Cookies on page 38.)

Be a Smart Cookie and Entertain Like One Too

Over the years, I've often wondered why the cookie swap has been relegated to Christmastime when it is one of the most gratifying and easy-to-plan parties around. Truthfully now, who can say they've ever received an invitation to a cookie swap in the summer? And who can give me one good reason why not? Anyone familiar with the party concept knows that the simple act of documenting and sharing prized family recipes sets this celebration apart.

But a cookie swap is more than warm and fuzzy. It is plain smart. As a specialized form of potluck, a cookie swap has all the same traits that make a potluck so effortless to host. Guests share in the baking and cost burden by bringing their favorite recipes. Music, games, and other activities can be minimized since the swapping of cookies is entertainment all by itself. The exchange of treats leads to more variety with less work. And, armed with goody baskets or boxes, your guests are sure to spotlessly clean up. The pluses are seemingly endless.

So why, then, do we reserve most of our entertaining for the holiday season when our calendars are already quite full? Or try to pull out all the stops, all by ourselves, when a cookie swap—a far simpler solution—will delight just as well? One thing is clear: it's high time to put the kibosh on this senseless Christmas-only cookie-swap trend.

In the pages that follow, I've assembled eight themed cookie parties that are designed to do precisely this. With a party for every season—and occasions as diverse as kids' birthdays and bridal showers—this book will show you how the joy of a special cookie swap can transcend the month of December to be shared with loved ones at any time of year.

Cook Up an Over-the-Top Swap

Although a cookie exchange is inherently easy to pull off, some ingenuity is required to plan one that will be unique and exciting. Hosting a swap in an atypical season such as spring, summer, or fall is a sure way to catch guests' attention. And once you've got their interest, it's not as difficult as you might think to hold it rapt. All you need is a little time and an eye for detail to push your swap over the top.

Should "over the top" make you anxious, take a deep breath. I do not mean "lavish" or "expensive." I simply mean that your party should contain some elements of surprise—an uncommon recipe or two, or a creative cookie display or design feature—that will dazzle partygoers without breaking the bank or tethering you to the kitchen. Over-the-top swaps are also high on handcrafted—and often inexpensive—touches. Perhaps your touch will be an invitation made from old family photos, or a decoupaged box filled with keepsake recipes? Over-the-top touches can come in many forms, but they have one characteristic in common: they always spring from the heart.

Select a Theme

To cook up an over-the-top swap, I begin by selecting a unifying theme to keep myself focused. Remember: since most guests' cookie swap experiences have been limited to Christmas, even a familiar theme such as a birthday or an anniversary can come across as new and different if set off with carefully selected cookies and party elements.

Also keep in mind that all-inclusive themes can be great fun. When I was growing up, cookie swaps were the pastime of women, but there's no reason dads and kids can't be included too. Everyone appreciates a good cookie, and baking for a swap is a wonderful way to expose children to the virtues of food made from scratch.

Cookie Swap Countdown

1. At least four weeks prior to the party:

- Choose a date and send out invitations to allow guests ample time to bake. Ask each guest to bring a favorite cookie and enough copies of the recipe for all to share.

- Though there are no hard-and-fast rules about how many cookies your guests should bring, consider capping each guest's contribution at five or six dozen (generally no more than two or three standard-sized batches), or at whatever number s/he can comfortably prepare. The goal is to keep the event stress-free for everyone.

- Most importantly, use the invitation to your guests' advantage. Identify any known food allergies in advance and broadcast off-limits ingredients in the invitation. If your event is themed, share the concept so guests can bake clever cookie tie-ins if they wish. You might even include a few tried-and-true recipes as inspiration.

2. With two to four weeks to go:

- Gather all the essential support for the cookies, such as serving plates (should guests forget them), napkins, beverages, and containers for packing up the take-home treats. Elevate your swap by avoiding paper plates and plastic wrap whenever you can.

- Stock up on paper and pencils for writing down recipes, making name tags for cookies, and/or listing the ingredients in each recipe. (The latter is especially important if guests have food allergies.)

3. With one to two weeks to go:

- Make your cookie contributions as close to the event as possible. If time won't permit last-minute preparation, choose cookies with a long shelf-life, or doughs that can withstand some freezing.

- It's best not to let fragile cookies dominate your offerings. If you opt for fragile cookies, gather the packaging and transport instructions that guests will need to get the cookies home in one piece. (As a general rule, package fragile cookies in one layer and cushion them with paper towels to prevent them from sliding in the car.)

- Set your table for the cookies it will soon receive.

4. On the day of the event:

- Welcome friends with open arms. After a few hours of lively conversation and cookie sampling, give everyone the signal to swap treats. Partygoers should take home nearly the same quantity of cookies as they brought, but their choices will now be immense.

Focus on the Defining Details

After the theme is set, the work of over-the-top party preparation really begins. More often than not, this is the time when hosts get overwhelmed. Should your head start spinning at this stage, I suggest you limit your investment to the few details that guests are most likely to remember and, therefore, savor. These defining details, as I like to call them, include what guests see first (the invitation), what they see last (the take-home cookie packaging), and the cookies, of course.

Trust me, you'll be well on your way to an over-the-top swap if you do three things. One, communicate the theme in the party invitation. Two, replace the usual—and not so attractive—paper plates and plastic wrap with a carrying container that fits the party concept. Three, put a seasonal or thematic twist on the cookies that you contribute to the mix. (The recipes in the following chapters do just this.)

If you have the time and desire to put your imprint on other details, I've included ideas for favors, décor, and cookie displays in each chapter. But mind you, these fine points are icing on the cake—or the cookie, that is.

Distinguish the Details

Once you've identified the details you plan to develop, it's time to unleash your creativity. Don't forget: your party is more likely to be over-the-top if the details stand out as meaningful expressions of yourself.

To get my creative juices flowing, I have a few tricks that I routinely pull out from under my sleeve. First, I try to personalize the party whenever I can. Working guests' names or photos into the favors or take-home packaging is an easy way to jazz up otherwise ordinary gifts. Plus, it is one of the most direct ways to make guests feel special. Repurposing is another useful trick, especially for generating unexpected cookie presentations. I start by making long lists of common objects related to the party theme and then try to find ways to use them in my cookie displays. In the tablescapes that open each chapter, you'll find all sorts of everyday items used in fun yet practical ways. Look closely, and you'll also see hints of my friends and family members, adding personality to the events.

For the ultimate thematic twist, I love to use cutout cookies as part of the décor or to replace other party elements. Cookies contribute color, flavor, texture, and fragrance, all at the same time. What's more, when cookies double as décor, you can often forego costly flowers, table accessories, and other party props. Sprinkled throughout the chapters, you'll discover edibles of every form—from cookie center-pieces and invitations to take-home boxes and baskets. Each chapter also contains a signature cutout cookie that showcases one or more of eleven distinct decorating techniques. Whether you choose to replicate these signature cookies and edible projects or to design your own, "Cookie-Cutter Approaches" (p. 142) provides all the tools to get you started. There you'll find the recipes that are the foundation of my cookie projects, such as Cutout Cookie Gingerbread, Signature Sugar Cookie Dough, and Royal Icing, and other basic recipes that I rely on more than once in the cookie swaps. "The Sugar on Top" (p. 152) provides added sweetness with step-by-step instructions for top-coating, marbling, outlining, and other decorating techniques.

How to Use This Book

The parties you are about to experience are fully loaded. Each one comes with a complete cookie menu and ideas for nearly every party element. While I hope these parties will be a rich source of inspiration, I also hope you will mix the projects and recipes to suit you—not just your personal style, but your skill level and available time as well.

To help my parties work for you, I've included several planning and preparation tools throughout the book. You'll find a key attached to each recipe that highlights complexity, active time, cookie type, and other preparation advice. (See "De-coding the Cookie Key," this page.) Optional decorating steps are also called out separately. If time is scarce, they can simply be skipped. As for guidance on nonedible crafts such as invitations, favors, and the like, look to "Stand-ins" for extra easy

and budget-friendly alternatives to my more challenging projects.

Finally, "Resources" (p. 156) is a guide to the less common ingredients and supplies used on occasion in the recipes. It includes contact information for purveyors of custom cookie cutters and stencils, unusual extracts and oils, dragées (sugar beads) and other ready-made cookie decorations, and various cookie-making tools.

To this point, I've given you a nibble of the parties that lie ahead. It's now time for a more substantial taste. Whether you devour this book in ravenous bites or stretch it out over days, I hope you enjoy the adventure.

De-coding the Cookie Key

- *Complexity* speaks only to the inherent challenge posed by the recipe, not to the required time.

1 Easy enough for the novice cook

2 Most average home cooks could make with no trouble

3 Best left to skilled home bakers or those seeking a challenge

- *Active Time* includes hands-on time from ingredient preparation through popping the cookie sheets into the oven; excludes baking, chilling, cooling, and optional decorating time. Active time is measured to the nearest quarter hour and ranges from ¼ hour to 2 or more hours.

Since this measure can vary tremendously with kitchen experience, it is best used to identify those recipes that are more or less time consuming than the norm.

- *Type* categorizes the cookie into one or more of seven classes. Check out the tips for each type starting on page 10.

- *Prep Talk* tells you what parts of a recipe need to be done in advance as well as how far ahead you can push the baking before there is a marked change in the cookie's flavor or texture. Storage tips and any special tools required are also noted here. Note: I generally don't like to bake more than 1 or 2 days ahead or to freeze pre-baked cookies, as most cookies are best the day they're made. However, some recipes require chilling, freezing, or other advance preparation, and others are more forgiving if you have no choice but to bake ahead.

THAT'S HOW THE COOKIE CRUMBLES

ead this chapter, and my cookies will never throw you any curve balls. Here you'll find specific tips to help you master each of the seven basic cookie types in this book, as well as general recommendations that apply to every recipe.

1. **Bar:** A cookie formed by baking the dough or batter in one large block in a baking or jelly-roll pan. The block is then cut into individual portions.

- Avoid using pans of a different size than specified. The size of the pan, and consequently the depth to which the batter fills the pan, can have a big impact on baking time and bar texture.

- To make the matter of pan size easy for you, I use only a few standard pans in this book: a 9 x 13 x 2-inch, a 9 x 9 x 2-inch, a 10 x 15 x 1-inch (also referred to as a jelly-roll pan), and a 10 x 15 x 2-inch pan (sometimes called a roasting pan and most often available in glass rather than metal).

- You may substitute pan types (i.e., glass for metal, or vice versa), but bars baked in glass will cook more quickly—all else being the same. If you substitute glass for metal, be sure to check the recipes for doneness a few minutes earlier than indicated.

Raspberry-Truffle Brownie Bars (recipe, p. 20).

- If you're sensitive to the aesthetics of what you eat, then never skip instructions for lining the pans. Lining with foil or parchment paper allows the bars to be removed from the pan in one block, without breakage. And with the pan out of the way, it's much easier to cut the block into neat portions.

- Smooth out any big wrinkles in foil-lined pans before you fill them. (Otherwise, the bars can bake into the wrinkles, making it harder to later remove the foil.) The easiest way to smooth wrinkles, and to "seat" the foil flush against the sides of the pan, is to gently press another pan of the same size into the one that's lined.

- Many of my bar recipes call for a crust that is pressed into the bottom of the pan. After pressing the crust, it's always a good idea to level it with a small offset spatula (see "FAQ," p. 146). The crust will bake more evenly this way; plus, the bars will be more uniform once cut.

- Trimming the cookie block before cutting it into smaller portions is completely optional. However, removing crusty, sloped edges will result in bars of more uniform shape and texture. *Note:* The yields in my recipes assume that all cookie blocks are trimmed before cutting.

- Bars will stay fresh longer if cut just before you plan to serve them. In the meantime, leave them uncut in the pan, tightly covered in foil. To keep cut edges from drying out, cover them with plastic wrap or parchment paper before covering the pan.

- For truly professional looking portions, cut the cookie block with a sharp knife wiped clean with a warm, damp cloth between slices. Don't slide the knife; instead, cut straight down by applying pressure on top of the blade. If a recipe requires cutting through solid chocolate (such as chocolate chips on top of bars), it helps to heat the knife over a hot stove burner before cutting.

2. **Drop:** A cookie formed by dropping the dough off a measuring spoon or by portioning it with a scoop. Drop cookies are great cookies for beginners, as they are arguably the easiest and quickest type to shape.

- For the sake of expediency, my recipes call for dropping the dough as soon as it is mixed. You can always make the dough in advance and chill it, but you need to be aware that the temperature of the dough will affect the shape and texture of the end cookie.

- Chilled dough tends to spread less than freshly mixed dough baked the same time; it will also bake to a softer texture. To achieve the results described in my recipes, it's best to bring chilled dough to room temperature before baking, unless otherwise specified.

- Portioning the dough with a round scoop, aka a disher, not only results in the most uniform cookies but is also quicker and less messy than portioning with measuring spoons. Dishers can be found in most kitchenware stores in sizes ranging from about 1 inch in diameter (1 teaspoon) to 2 ¾ inches in diameter (8 tablespoons). You may also find disher size referred to on a numerical scale—#100 corresponding to the smallest and #8 to the largest. For instance, a round #30 disher—a size commonly used for big cookies—is 1⅞ inches in diameter, or about 2 tablespoons. **Stand-in:** If you don't own a disher, my recipes always provide a measuring-spoon equivalent.

- In addition to being very easy, drop cookies are also incredibly accommodating. If you like the basic dough but would rather substitute other mix-ins (nuts, chocolate chips, dried fruit, or something else that moves you), feel free. As long as you don't alter the ingredients that make up the dough, a winning variation is virtually guaranteed.

3. Hand-shaped: A cookie formed in whole, or in part, by shaping it with your hands. These cookies are often hybrids, insofar as the dough might first be dropped or rolled before the hand-shaping takes place.

- The key to a nicely formed hand-shaped cookie is, ironically, not to handle it too much. The warmth of your hands will quickly soften the dough, especially one with a high butter content, making it sticky and difficult to shape. As a general rule, work quickly and clean your hands regularly with cold tap water to keep them cool and damp. (Dough is less likely to cling to slightly damp hands.)

- Dusting your hands lightly with flour can also prevent sticking. However, only dust them if dampening does not work, or if the recipe specifically instructs you to do so, as excess flour can have a drying and toughening effect on the dough.

- If even after dampening and dusting your hands, the dough is too

For Every Cookie Recipe . . .

- **Look before you leap.** To save time in the long run, read the recipe from start to finish before you start, and measure and prep all ingredients as they're described in the ingredient list. Some recipes call for toasted and cooled nuts, others for softened butter, etc.

- **Heed orders.** Pay attention to the order of operations in the ingredient list. Any operation, such as "sifted" or "chopped," that is listed after the ingredient should be performed after that ingredient is measured. For instance, if a recipe calls for "1 cup flour, sifted," you should sift the flour after measuring it. If, instead, the recipe calls for "1 cup sifted flour," you should sift before measuring. In the latter case, you'll end up with less flour by weight. Though this distinction may seem minor, the difference of even an ounce of flour can have a large impact on the texture and moistness of baked goods.

- **Mind your measures.** In baking, winging measurements rarely works. To make my recipes come out just as I intended, always measure dry ingredients by spooning them into the measuring cup and leveling the top with a straight-sided spatula or knife. Plunging the measuring cup into the flour bin compresses the flour, which will leave you with more flour by weight than desired—and, in turn, a heavier, drier product.

- **Don't take sides.** If your cookie sheet has sides of any height, turn it over and bake on the back. This way, the cookies will bake at closer to the same rate. (Because metal is an efficient heat conductor, cookies that flank the sides of the cookie sheet will brown more rapidly than those in the middle.) It's also easier to slide the cookies onto cooling racks when there are no sides to get in the way.

- **Bulk up.** Use large (13 x 18-inch) heavy-gauge aluminized-steel jelly-roll pans for cookie sheets whenever you can. The light-colored, thick metal surface encourages uniform browning, and the reinforced rim minimizes warping of the pan over time. Plus, the generous size accommodates more cookies.

- **Give your cookies space.** To ensure even baking and browning, don't crowd the cookies on the cookie sheet, bake one sheet at a time in the center of the oven (unless otherwise specified), and rotate the sheet midway through baking, if needed.

sticky to easily handle, chill the dough until it is workable. Chilling is preferable to dusting the dough and introducing excess flour.

- For cookies that get shaped into balls, I recommend portioning the dough with a disher (p. 11) before you roll it between your palms. You can always portion the dough with your hands if you prefer, but it is harder to control cookie size this way.

4. Icebox: A cookie where the dough is shaped into logs, frozen, and then cut crosswise into slices before baking. Different methods of coloring and shaping the dough can lead to a variety of cookie patterns.

- For the neatest, most precise patterns, pay close attention to chilling time. Icebox cookie dough is often chilled both before and after it is shaped into logs.

- Chilling time prior to shaping will depend on your refrigerator temperature and the softness of your dough, as often determined by the softness of the butter in it. As a guideline, chill the dough 1 to 2 hours before shaping. If shaping involves rolling the dough into thin sheets (i.e., with Pinwheel and Pinstripe, p. 145), chill the dough closer to 2 hours, or until very firm. To accelerate the chilling process, you can freeze the dough, but watch it closely. It can quickly get too firm to easily shape.

- To avoid sticking, roll and shape the dough on a floured surface, adding flour only as you need it. Because the butter content of icebox dough is high, the dough can rapidly soften as you work with it. For easier handling at any stage of the process, simply re-chill the dough. (Chilling is always better than adding more flour, as excess flour will make the dough pasty and tough.)

- If shaping involves piecing together different colors of icebox dough, as with the shaping variations shown on page 145, be sure to dust excess flour off the dough before joining the pieces. For added security, stick the pieces to one another with a light coating of egg wash (1 egg white lightly beaten with 2 teaspoons water).

- Once you've formed the logs, wrap them tightly in plastic to hold their shape. Freeze 1 to 2 hours, or until the dough is quite solid but still sliceable without requiring a lot of force. Stand round logs on end in the freezer to prevent them from flattening on one side.

5. Pressed (or Piped): A cookie that is given a distinctive shape by forcing the dough through a cookie press fitted with a special disk or decorative tip (or by piping the batter with a pastry bag fitted with a decorative tip.) The beauty of these cookies is that they hold their interesting shapes even after they're baked.

- The tool for this task—cookie press or pastry bag—depends on the stiffness of the cookie dough or batter. The stiffer the dough, the better suited it is for a cookie press. (Either tool can be found in kitchenware or cake decorating supply stores.)

- In this book, most of the pressed cookies use a relatively stiff dough made with a large proportion of flour to fat and more shortening than butter. (This formula keeps the cookies from spreading and losing their shape in the heat of the oven. Shortening also imparts a crispy tenderness that isn't achievable with 100 percent butter.) In these cases, the dough is generally too thick to comfortably press through a pastry bag; the extra leverage of a cookie press is often needed.

- Cookie presses load and operate slightly differently from manufacturer to manufacturer. Read the manufacturer's instructions carefully before working with your press.

- Most of the piped cookies in this book, including Friendly Ghosts, Top Dogs, and Chocolate-Chai Burgers, call for meringue, a mixture of egg whites and sugar beaten to fluffy peaks. This soft "batter" is easily—and best—piped through a pastry bag. Do not use a cookie press; you will only deflate the whites when trying to fit them into the narrow cookie press chamber.

- Whether you're working with a stiff dough or a meringue, you should press or pipe the mixture as soon as it is ready. Avoid chilling dough, as time in the fridge will only make it stiffer and more difficult to press. Chilling can also cause the dough to crack when pushed through the press. If you must make the dough in advance, then chill it. But be sure to wrap it tightly in plastic so it doesn't dry out and to bring it to room temperature before pressing.

- With meringue, you not only have to use it right away, but you must also work quickly. If meringue sits too long at room temperature, it will deflate and not hold a well-defined shape.

- If you're working with a recipe that calls for holding the cookie press at a 90-degree angle to the cookie sheet (as in Pink Spritz Daisy Cookies), it is best not to prep the sheet in any way. The cookies will not stick as readily to a greased or parchment paper-lined pan, and, therefore, may not separate from the press. (*Note:* You will not experience this problem with cookies that call for holding the cookie press at a 45-degree angle to the pan.)

6. Rolled: A cookie formed by rolling the dough into a large thin sheet and then cutting it with a knife, pastry wheel, or cookie cutter into decorative shapes.

- Always refrigerate rolled cookie dough before you work with it. Flatten the dough into one or more disks (each about ½ inch thick) and wrap each disk tightly in plastic before setting in the fridge. Flattening the dough will expedite the chilling process and ensure that the dough chills evenly. (You can also freeze the dough to further speed up the process. In this case, flatten the dough into ¼-inch-thick disks to ensure even chilling.)

- Chilling time will vary with the amount of butter in the dough, the softness of the butter at the time the dough was mixed, and the temperature of your refrigerator. Use the instructions for chilling time in each recipe as a guideline, but always follow the cues given by the dough (see below).

- If the dough cracks or requires a lot of pressure to roll (cue #1), you have probably chilled it too long. Let it soften at room temperature until it is more workable. Conversely, if the dough sticks to the rolling pin or work surface even after dusting them with flour (cue #2), the dough is too soft and needs more chilling.

- There is no reason to roll between plastic or to use a pastry cloth or sleeve to prevent sticking, especially if the dough has been properly chilled. A light flouring of your work surface and rolling pin is usually enough. (In addition to being cumbersome to handle, pastry cloths and plastic can also leave wrinkles in the dough.) *Note:* The one exception to this rule is Anise-Scented Springerle. It is a unique form of rolled cookie that is embossed with a decorative mold or rolling pin. For the best imprints, you may need to generously dust both the work surface and mold (or rolling pin) with flour.

- As you roll, stop on occasion to make sure the underside of the dough isn't stuck to the work surface. When gently pushed, the dough should slide freely. If it doesn't, carefully lift up the corners and lightly dust underneath with flour.

- For the neatest looking cutouts, always clean any dough off the cookie cutter before using it. If your dough is especially soft, you may also want to lightly dust the cutter with flour to prevent the dough from sticking.

- To minimize distortion of cut cookies, move them from the work surface to the cookie sheet with a large offset spatula. For very large cookies that aren't easily transferred with a spatula, slide the sheet of rolled dough onto the cookie sheet and cut directly on top of the pan. Remove excess dough from around the cookies before baking.

- Avoid moving the cookies once they have been set on the cookie sheet. Most dough will soften quickly once rolled; any extra handling will only result in misshapen cookies.

- Dough scraps can always be re-rolled. To keep the dough from getting dry and pasty, brush off any excess flour before re-rolling. And chill the dough again if needed.

7. Sandwich: Two cookie layers that surround a soft, often perishable filling, such as ganache, buttercream, or jam.

- For this cookie-within-a-cookie, you must pay attention to two sets of tips—these guidelines for sandwiches as well as those for the type of cookie that surrounds the filling. Rolled, drop, and pressed (or piped) cookies are the types I most frequently use in sandwiches.

- Since sandwich fillings are often soft and perishable, I like to fill the cookies within a few hours of serving. When filled too soon or refrigerated too long, the crunchy cookie layers soften. If you prefer a softer cookie, then, by all means, fill the cookies sooner. But to me, the interplay of crunchy cookie and soft filling is what makes sandwiches so appealing.

- Likewise, perishable fillings, such as ganache and buttercream, are best made as they are needed. If made far in advance of sandwich assembly, these fillings should be refrigerated, but once refrigerated, they set to a firm, hard-to-spread consistency. To be usable, they must be slowly brought to room temperature, preferably with no application of direct heat—a process that takes a few hours.

Peanut Butter and Jelly Sandwiches (recipe, p. 106).

AN AFFAIR OF THE HEART

There's no better way to woo your special someone than with this stylish cookie swap, a couples' affair in celebration of Valentine's Day. With an abundance of chocolate, flowers (albeit cookie ones), and love notes passing in unexpected places, this party combines the best of what the holiday traditionally offers with contemporary flair. If you're looking for a soft touch, you won't find it here. This swap is an ardent embrace, grabbing guests with its high-voltage hues, adult ingredients, and of-the-moment party favors.

The romance starts with the invitation—oversized heart cookies delivered to guests in velvet-trimmed candy boxes. The courtship unfolds at the event, where guests are seduced by a bevy of cookies owing their appeal to intoxicating liqueurs and proven aphrodisiacs such as chocolate, figs, and berries. Other cookies win guests over with their thematic styling. Colorful bouquets of heart cookies pop from gumball-filled vases, and flashes of fiery paper sneak out of Valentine fortune cookies, teasing guests with predictions of love, fulfilled and unrequited.

As this tête-à-tête with sweets draws to a close, guests receive CDs burned with the party's recipes and chic red shadow boxes filled with cookies—two touches completely in sync with the party's modern theme. Heartache is sure to follow the end of this affair, but these lovely gestures are the perfect cure.

Cause to Celebrate:
Valentine's Day, an engagement, a special anniversary, a bridal shower, a birthday for the romantic at heart, a reunion of loved ones.

Clockwise from top, Chocolate-Fig Oatmeal Bars, Raspberry-Truffle Brownie Bars, Brown Sugar–Pecan Sweethearts, and Sweet Note-things. Not pictured: Brandied Cherry–Chocolate Sin Cookies.

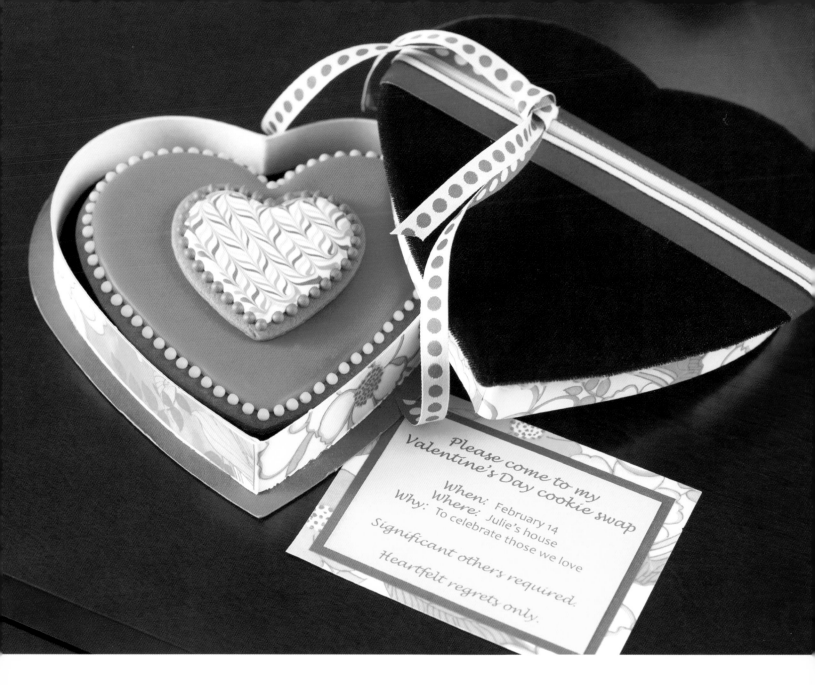

Please come to my
Valentine's Day cookie swap

When: February 14
Where: Julie's house
Why: To celebrate those we love

Significant others required.

Heartfelt regrets only.

Gingerbread Valentine Invitations

To make: Adhere decorative papers to fit the tops and sides of heart-shaped candy boxes using spray adhesive. For fabric-covered lids, mount the fabric first with spray adhesive and then tack the edges under the lid using a glue gun. Heavier trims and ribbons are best tacked with a glue gun as well.

Bake Cutout Cookie Gingerbread hearts (p. 146) and decorate as desired (see Royal Icing, p. 151, and cookie decorating techniques, p. 152). Place the cookies in the boxes and then again in padded envelopes before mailing. The party's date and time can be written with Royal Icing directly on the face of large hearts or printed on a paper insert or a ribbon tied to the box.

On Cloud Nine

To make: Fill a large (6- to 8-inch-diameter) vase with gumballs, sanding sugar, chocolate chips, jelly beans, or foil-covered chocolate hearts, and set a larger Styrofoam disk on top. It will be easier to apply the cotton candy to the disk if the disk is elevated and stationary.

Because cotton candy quickly attracts moisture, clouds are best assembled a few hours before party time. Secure large tufts of candy to the disk with toothpicks, handling the candy as little as possible to keep it from matting.

Nestle decorated heart and cupid cookies in the clouds; then set the vases out to be seen—and tasted! Just remember to tell guests to remove all toothpicks before eating any of the candy. (See page 156 for gumball and cotton candy sources.)

Bottom left: Why splurge on red roses when cookie bouquets can serve as both party décor and party favor? Fix cookie hearts onto the ends of long twigs with thick Royal Icing and arrange them in tall vases on your table. When it's time to say farewell, tie up the flowers with ribbon and offer up one lovely bunch to each guest.

Top left: Shadow boxes ordinarily used to display photos and keepsakes provide a captivating view of cookies, especially when jazzed with shiny red paint and personalized name plates.

Top right: Marbled cookies, such as these hearts, have all the appeal of intricate Italian endpapers found in fancy books. Though they may look complicated, they aren't the least bit time-consuming. For marbling technique details, see page 152.

Bottom right: Burn the swap's recipes onto punchy pink CDs and wrap them as take-home gifts in jewel cases spiffed up with polka-dotted papers and striped ribbons. Recipes can also be written on note cards backed with flashy papers and tucked into envelopes decorated with the same (pictured back).

Raspberry-Truffle Brownie Bars

Makes 2 dozen (1¾- to 2-inch) squares

In this triple-decker brownie, the season's favorite aphrodisiac factors into three places: a buttery crumb crust, a dense chocolate-raspberry filling, and a glossy ganache on top. *Note:* This brownie is only moderately sweet, so it is best reserved for adults.

Complexity:

Active Time:

Type:

Bar

Prep Talk: Store unglazed brownies at room temperature up to 4 to 5 days. Keep them covered (and uncut) in the pan until ready to glaze. Once glazed, the brownies must be refrigerated. (The glaze is perishable.) Because the brownie layer will harden if refrigerated too long, the glaze is best applied 1½ to 2 hours before serving. The brownies will be softest and most flavorful if served at room temperature.

Cocoa Shortbread Crust

1½ cups plus 3 tablespoons all-purpose flour

½ cup sifted superfine sugar

3 tablespoons unsweetened Dutch-process cocoa powder

¼ teaspoon salt

¾ cup (1½ sticks) unsalted butter, softened

1 large egg yolk

Raspberry Brownie Filling

¼ cup (½ stick) plus 2 tablespoons unsalted butter, cut into tablespoon-size pieces

6 ounces premium semisweet chocolate (see "FAQ," p. 150), finely chopped

2¼ ounces premium unsweetened chocolate, finely chopped
½ cup sifted superfine sugar
3 large eggs, room temperature, lightly beaten
4½ tablespoons Chambord or other premium raspberry liqueur
1½ teaspoons pure vanilla extract
¾ cup all-purpose flour

¾ cup seedless red raspberry jam, stirred to loosen (for topping)

Raspberry Truffle Glaze
½ recipe Ganache (p. 149), chocolate increased to 8 ounces and
    corn syrup increased to 1 tablespoon
1 tablespoon Chambord or other premium raspberry liqueur

Decoration (optional)
About 2 ounces premium milk chocolate, melted

1. Position a rack in the middle of the oven and preheat the oven to
350 degrees F. Line the bottom and sides of a 9 x 13 x 2-inch baking pan with foil, leaving a 1-inch overhang around the top edge of
the pan. Lightly coat the foil with nonstick cooking spray.

2. Mix the Cocoa Shortbread Crust. Combine the flour, superfine
sugar, cocoa powder, and salt in a medium bowl. Using a fork or
your hands, work in the butter and egg yolk until the mixture is
uniformly moistened but crumbly. (There should be no dry spots.)
Press the dough into an even ¼-inch layer on the bottom of the
prepared pan.

3. Bake the crust 14 to 15 minutes, or until dull on top and slightly
puffy but still soft. Do not overbake. Transfer to a wire rack while
you prepare the filling.

4. Prepare the Raspberry Brownie Filling. Combine the butter, semisweet chocolate, and unsweetened chocolate in the top of a double
boiler set over barely simmering water. Stir as needed until the
chocolate and butter are just melted. Remove from heat and gently
whisk in the superfine sugar, followed by the eggs, Chambord, and

vanilla extract. Stir in the flour, mixing just until smooth and shiny.
(Do not overmix, or the batter may break.) Pour the batter on top
of the crust and spread into an even layer with a small offset spatula
(see "FAQ," p. 146).

5. Spoon the jam evenly over the top. With a small offset spatula,
spread it into a thin layer that completely covers the brownie filling.

6. Bake the brownies about 20 minutes. Do not overbake. When
done, the brownies will be set through to the middle and slightly
puffed around the edges. A cake tester inserted into the center will
come out with very damp crumbs on it. Transfer to a wire rack and
cool completely before glazing or storing. (The brownie will set
further upon cooling.)

7. Prepare and apply the Raspberry Truffle Glaze. Prepare ½ recipe
Ganache, increasing the chocolate to 8 ounces and the corn
syrup to 1 tablespoon. Stir in the Chambord at the end. Pour the
ganache evenly over the brownie. Gently tilt or shake the pan so
the ganache completely coats the top.

8. Decorate (optional). For a marbled top, work quickly while the
ganache is still fluid. Fill a parchment pastry cone (p. 153) with the
melted milk chocolate. Pipe thin lines ¼ to ½ inch apart across the
ganache. Draw a toothpick (or cake tester) back and forth through
the chocolate and ganache to create a marbled pattern.

9. Set the pan in the refrigerator for 1½ to 2 hours, or until the
ganache is firm enough to cleanly cut. (Do not overchill or the
brownies will harden.)

10. Remove the brownies from the pan in one block by gently pulling up
on the foil overhang, and place directly on a cutting board. Remove
all foil and trim any uneven edges before cutting the block into 1¾- to
2-inch squares. For the neatest cuts, slice the bars while the ganache
is firm and wipe the knife clean with a warm, damp cloth between
slices. Serve at room temperature.

Sweet Note-things

Makes 4 to 4½ dozen (2-inch folded) cookies

These delicate cocoa tuiles—complete with an espresso-powder kick—are shaped fortune cookie–style around a sweet sentiment. *Note:* The batter is a breeze to mix; however, the cookie folding may take some practice. It is especially important to shape the cookies directly from the oven and to work quickly before they set.

Complexity:	Active Time:	Type:
3	⏰ ⏰	Drop; hand-shaped

Prep Talk: Silicone baking mats are recommended for this recipe, though nonstick cookie sheets can be substituted (see Step 1, next page). These cookies are especially vulnerable to humidity, so for

the crispiest results, bake on a dry, sunny day   and package
the cookies as soon as they've cooled. Store the cookies in airtight
containers at room temperature up to 1 week.

¾ cup plus 2 tablespoons all-purpose flour

2 tablespoons unsweetened Dutch-process cocoa powder

¼ teaspoon salt

1 cup sifted superfine sugar

1½ teaspoons instant espresso powder

4 large egg whites, room temperature

¼ cup (½ stick) plus 1 tablespoon unsalted butter, melted and cooled
    to lukewarm

3 tablespoons heavy cream

¾ teaspoon coffee extract (p. 156)

¼ teaspoon pure vanilla extract

4 to 4½ dozen love notes, printed on slender strips of paper
    (1 per cookie)

1. Position a rack in the center of the oven and preheat the oven
   to 400 degrees F. Line two or more cookie sheets with silicone
   baking mats. You may also use nonstick cookie sheets, though
   the cookies will bake more quickly on them, especially if they are
   dark. A dark pan can also make it more difficult to determine when
   these dark cookies are properly browned. (*Note:* With nonstick
   cookie sheets, no pan preparation is necessary. The cookies tend
   to misshape on parchment paper and will get doughy if baked on
   greased and floured pans.)

2. Sift the flour, cocoa powder, and salt together in a small bowl. Set
   aside for use in Step 4.

3. Combine the superfine sugar and espresso powder in the bowl of an
   electric mixer fitted with a whip attachment. (See "Stand-in," p. 142.)
   Add the egg whites. Beat on medium speed until the whites are
   frothy and the espresso powder has completely dissolved. Gradually add the melted butter and cream. Beat until well combined.

4. Turn the mixer to low speed and slowly add the flour mixture, beating just until smooth. Scrape down the sides of the bowl and stir in
   the extracts.

5. Drop the batter onto the prepared (or nonstick) cookie sheets
   using a scant 1⅜-inch (#70) scoop, or about 2 level teaspoons
   batter per cookie. Place no more than three or four cookies on
   each cookie sheet. (*Note:* Because the cookies must be shaped
   while they are warm, it is best not to bake too many at once.) Using
   the back of a small spoon, spread each mound into a circle about
   3½ to 3¾ inches in diameter. (For the most uniform circle, move
   the spoon in ever increasing circles until the cookie reaches the
   proper size.) The cookies should be quite thin; however, you should
   not see through them to the baking mat (or nonstick cookie sheet).
   Carefully smooth the cookies with a small offset spatula to even out
   any heavy or thin spots.

6. Bake 5 to 7 minutes, or until set and slightly darkened around the
   edges. Watch carefully, as the cookies go from done to burned in a
   flash.

7. Shape into fortune cookies. Work quickly before the cookies set.
   Shape one cookie at a time, leaving the others on the cookie sheet
   so they stay warm and pliable. Place a love note along the center of
   the cookie. Fold the cookie loosely in half, leaving a pocket around
   the note. The cookie should not be folded flat. (If the cookie col-
   lapses onto itself, it is either too warm or wasn't baked long enough.
   Let it cool for a few seconds and try shaping it again. If it still col-
   lapses, return the cookies to the oven to briefly bake.) Press your
   forefinger into the folded side of the cookie while pulling the two
   ends of the cookie around your forefinger with your other hand.
   Remove your forefinger while still holding the ends together. Hold
   the cookie until it cools just enough to keep its shape. Transfer to a
   wire rack and repeat with the remaining cookies. Cool completely
   before storing.

Brandied Cherry-Chocolate Sin Cookies

Makes about 2 dozen (2¼- to 2½-inch) cookies

Inspired by a recipe in Alice Medrich's *Cookies and Brownies* (1999), this voluptuous chocolate cookie has been enhanced with cocoa, brown sugar, and brandy-soaked cherries. *Note:* For a more kid-friendly version, omit the cognac and add the cherries unsoaked.

Complexity:	Active Time:	Type:
		Drop

Prep Talk: Store in airtight containers at room temperature for 5 to 7 days. *Note:* The chocolate on top will look its best if applied just before serving. It can turn dull and streaky if stored at temperatures in excess of 65 to 70 degrees F or under humid conditions.

½ cup fine cognac
¾ cup dried tart cherries
8 ounces premium semisweet chocolate, finely chopped
2 tablespoons unsalted butter
¼ cup all-purpose flour
2 teaspoons unsweetened Dutch-process cocoa powder
¼ teaspoon baking powder
⅛ teaspoon salt
2 large eggs, room temperature
¼ cup plus 2 tablespoons granulated sugar
2 tablespoons firmly packed light brown sugar
1½ teaspoons cherry extract
½ teaspoon pure vanilla extract
2 cups pecan halves, lightly toasted, cooled, and chopped
¾ cup premium milk chocolate chips

Decoration (optional)
About 2 ounces premium bittersweet chocolate, melted

1. Warm the cognac in a small saucepan over medium heat. Remove from the heat and add the dried cherries. Let the cherries soak in the cognac about 30 minutes.

2. Position a rack in the middle of the oven and preheat the oven to 350 degrees F. Line two or more cookie sheets with parchment paper.

3. Place the chocolate and butter in the top of a double boiler over barely simmering water. Stir until melted; then cool to lukewarm. Set aside for use in Step 6.

4. Combine the flour, cocoa powder, baking powder, and salt in a small bowl. Set aside for use in Step 7.

5. Drain the cherries and discard all but 2 teaspoons of the cognac.

6. Whisk the eggs, sugars, extracts, and 2 teaspoons cognac together in a large bowl. Gradually add the chocolate mixture. Whisk until combined.

7. Stir in the flour mixture, followed by the pecans, chocolate chips, and drained cherries.

8. Portion the dough into mounds using a level 1⅞-inch (#30) scoop, or 1 heaping tablespoon per mound, and place the mounds 1 to 2 inches apart on the prepared cookie sheets. Be sure to portion the cookies while the chocolate is still fluid. The cookies will be easier to drop and will have a more interesting and textured appearance this way.

9. Bake 13 to15 minutes for a crisp outside and soft inside, or longer for a firmer cookie through and through. Cool 1 to 2 minutes on the cookie sheets before transferring to wire racks. Cool completely before storing.

10. Decorate (optional). Just before serving, drizzle with melted bittersweet chocolate. Place the cookies briefly in the fridge, just long enough to allow the chocolate to set, and serve.

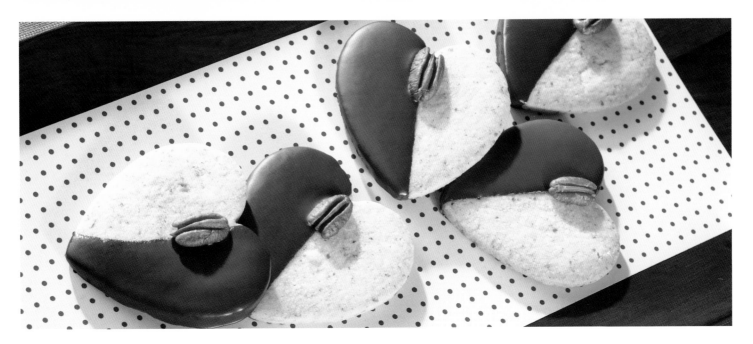

Brown Sugar–Pecan Sweethearts
Makes about 2 ½ dozen (2 ¼ x 2 ½- to 2 ¾-inch) hearts

Hearts—plain shortbread ones, that is—are warmed with rich caramel accents of pecans and brown sugar in this meltingly delicious variation of Shortbread, Straight Up.

Complexity:	Active Time:	Type:
1		Rolled

Prep Talk: The dough must be chilled 1 to 2 hours before rolling and cutting. The dough can be frozen up to 1 month with minimal loss of flavor if wrapped tightly in plastic and then foil. Store baked cookies in airtight containers at room temperature no longer than 2 weeks. *Note:* The dipping chocolate will look its best if applied just before serving. It can turn dull and streaky if stored at temperatures in excess of 65 to 70 degrees F or under humid conditions.

1 recipe Shortbread, Straight Up (p. 143), almonds, granulated sugar, and powdered sugar omitted

1 cup pecan halves

½ cup firmly packed light brown sugar

Decoration (optional)

1 pound premium semisweet or bittersweet chocolate, melted (for dipping)

About 2½ dozen pecan halves (1 per cookie)

1. Prepare 1 recipe Shortbread, Straight Up, replacing the almonds with the pecans, and the granulated and powdered sugar with the brown sugar.

2. Chill and roll the dough as instructed on page 143, but cut the dough into hearts with a 2 ¼ x 2 ½- to 2 ¾-inch heart cutter. If you plan to decorate the cookies with chocolate in Step 3, below, omit the sugar for sprinkling on the cookie tops. Bake and cool as directed on page 143 before dipping in chocolate or storing.

3. Decorate (optional). Pour the melted chocolate into a small (6- to 7-inch-diameter) bowl to at least a 1-inch depth. Dip half of each cookie in the chocolate. Gently shake off any excess chocolate and then wipe the cookie bottom clean by dragging it along the edge of the bowl. (This will prevent a "foot" of chocolate from pooling around the cookie.) Place the cookie on a parchment paper–lined cookie sheet and repeat with the remaining cookies. Before the chocolate sets, place a pecan half in the top center of each heart. Do not let the cookies sit at room temperature for an extended period, or the chocolate can get dull and streaky. As soon as one sheet is full, set it in the fridge about 10 minutes, just until the chocolate is firm. Serve immediately, if possible, or store as directed above.

    Note: There will be some leftover chocolate. Remove any crumbs by straining the chocolate through a sieve; then cover tightly and store at room temperature for another use.

Chocolate-Fig Oatmeal Bars

Makes 2 dozen (1¾- to 2-inch) squares

If rich, chocolate, and decadent sound seductive, then these moist fig bars, studded with chocolate chips and oatmeal streusel, will have you at first bite.

Complexity:

2

Active Time:

Type:

Bar

Prep Talk: These bars are great keepers. If stored in airtight containers at room temperature, they will taste as fresh on week two as they did on day one.

Chocolate-Fig Filling

1 cup coarsely chopped dried figs (preferably black Mission figs, stems removed)

1 cup coarsely chopped dried pitted dates (stems removed)

About 2 cups warm water, enough to cover dried fruit

3 tablespoons firmly packed light brown sugar

2 tablespoons fine cognac

1½ tablespoons finely grated orange zest

1 teaspoon ground cinnamon

½ teaspoon freshly grated nutmeg

½ teaspoon ground cloves

1 cup premium semisweet chocolate chips, divided

Oatmeal Streusel Crust (and Topping)

2¾ cups quick-cook oats

2 cups all-purpose flour

1 teaspoon baking powder

1 teaspoon salt

2 cups firmly packed light brown sugar

1 cup (2 sticks) unsalted butter, softened

2 large eggs

2 teaspoons pure orange extract

1 teaspoon pure vanilla extract

1 cup pecan halves, lightly toasted, cooled, and coarsely chopped

1. Position a rack in the center of the oven and preheat the oven to 350 degrees F. Line a 9 x 13 x 2-inch baking pan with a double layer of foil, leaving a 1-inch overhang around the top edge of the pan. Smooth out any big wrinkles in the foil and then lightly coat the foil with nonstick cooking spray.

2. Prepare the Chocolate-Fig Filling. Place the figs and dates in a medium (3-quart) saucepan and cover with warm water. Bring to a boil over medium-high heat, reduce the heat to medium-low, and simmer, uncovered, until the fruit is quite soft, about 15 minutes. Thoroughly drain the fruit and blot dry with paper towels. Pat the fruit into a ½-inch-thick layer on several paper towels. Top with more paper towels, and let the mixture sit about 10 minutes to allow the towels to absorb excess moisture. While the fruit is drying, proceed to Step 3 to prepare the streusel.

   Place the fruit in the bowl of a food processor fitted with a metal blade. Add the brown sugar, cognac, orange zest, and spices, and process about 30 seconds, or until the mixture is reduced to a smooth paste. Turn into a clean bowl, cool completely, and then stir in ½ cup chocolate chips.

3. Mix the Oatmeal Streusel Crust (and Topping). Combine the oats, flour, baking powder, and salt in a large bowl. Set aside.

   Combine the brown sugar and butter in the bowl of an electric mixer fitted with a paddle attachment. Beat on medium speed until smooth and creamy, about 1 minute. Add the eggs one at a time, beating well and scraping down the sides of the bowl after each addition. Beat another 30 seconds; then stir in the extracts by hand, followed by the dry ingredients. Mix just until there are no dry spots. Stir in the pecans.

4. Assemble the bars. Press about two-thirds of the streusel into the bottom of the prepared pan and reserve the remainder. (The crust should be an even ¼- to ⅜-inch thickness.) Spread the filling evenly over the crust. Drop the remaining streusel by heaping tablespoons on top to create a cobbled effect; then sprinkle with the rest of the chocolate chips.

5. Bake about 40 minutes, or until the streusel is golden brown and dry to the touch. Transfer to a wire rack and cool completely in the pan. (If the cookies are not cooled completely, they may be difficult to cut.)

6. Remove the cookies in one block by gently pulling up on the foil overhang or by easing the block out with an offset spatula. Place directly on a cutting board and remove all foil. Trim any uneven edges before cutting the block into 1¾- to 2-inch squares. For the neatest cuts, use a sharp knife wiped clean with a warm, damp cloth between slices. (If the chocolate chips are difficult to cut, heat the knife blade directly over a hot burner before cutting.)

SPRING FLING

Now here's a party that will put spring in your step—and just in time for the Easter holiday. If jellybeans and foil-covered chocolate eggs no longer strike you as interesting Easter basket fare, you're in the right place. At this swap, cookies double as birds' nests, rabbits, and spring bonnets, offering plenty of creative alternatives to bland mass-produced sweets.

Children will love the many fanciful details, from the invitation—a set of nested egg-boxes—to the gingerbread butterflies and cookie cobblestone trail. For added amusement, there are cookies galore just waiting to be turned into kids' projects and games. Stage a tabletop Easter egg hunt by concealing egg-shaped cookies deep in the wheat grass, or set out nonpareils, fondant, and a rainbow of icing colors, and let everyone decorate his or her own shortbread Easter hats.

The parting gift, a gingerbread basket complete with edible handle and bow, is one project that's clearly designed for the seasoned baker. Even so, kids will happily lend a hand—especially if "helping" means sneaking a piece of the cookie basket now and again.

Cause to Celebrate:
Easter; a springtime birthday, especially for the younger set (kids will adore all of the cute cookie rabbits and marshmallow chicks); the arrival of spring; just for the fun of it.

Clockwise from upper left nest: Bunny Trail Mix Cookies, Lemon-Poppy Seed Cottontail Cookies, Shortbread Easter Bonnets, and Kataifi Birds' Nests, along with gingerbread bunnies and butterflies. Not pictured: Pink Spritz Daisy Cookies and Quick Cutout Marshmallow Peeps.

Hop on over to my Easter
April 9, 3pm
Attendance eggs-pected. Regret

Nested Egg Invitations *(opposite)*

To make: Purchase egg-shaped papier-mâché boxes (available online) in three sizes. Three eggs, one of each size, will make up each invitation. Work with one egg at a time. Lightly coat the outside with spray adhesive and cover with crepe paper. (Crepe paper stretches and conforms well to the rounded egg surfaces.) Use a glue gun to secure ribbons and other trims to the edges. Slip a tiny cookie and invitation into the smallest egg before nesting the three eggs together.

3-D Gingerbread Butterflies

To make: Cut out Construction Gingerbread (pp. 146–147) or Cutout Cookie Gingerbread (p. 146) using your favorite butterfly cutter. (Large butterflies will hold up better if made from Construction Gingerbread.) Before baking, cut each butterfly in half lengthwise to separate the wings. Bake and cool as directed. Use Royal Icing to decorate the wings in pairs, making each wing a mirror image of its partner. (These butterflies' wings have been marbled and then accented with beadwork. See pages 152–153 for technique details.) When the cookies have dried completely, arrange matched wings together on parchment paper–lined cookie sheets.

Work with one set of wings at a time. Leave one wing lying flat on the cookie sheet, and prop the other with paper towels so it sits at an angle to the first. (The wings should be touching in the center.) Fill a parchment pastry cone with thick Royal Icing and cut a 1/8- to 1/4-inch hole in the tip. Create the butterfly "body" by piping a series of large icing dots through the center where the wings meet. Be sure the icing touches both wings, as, once dried, it will hold the wings together. Repeat with the remaining butterflies. Dry completely; then carefully lift the butterflies off the parchment paper, using a thin-bladed knife to loosen them first.

Optional: Glue the butterflies onto budding branches with thick Royal Icing, or embellish bare branches with fondant leaves (p. 155), as pictured left. Let the icing dry completely before moving the branches.

Stand-ins

For no-bake take-home containers in the spring theme, consider . . .

Opposite, top: Sanding (the process of applying decorative sugar or nonpareils to cookies) is one of the quickest ways to add sparkle and texture. These bunnies' tails and tummies have gone from flat to fluffy with white nonpareils. For sanding technique details, check out page 154.

Opposite, bottom: Organizing the day's spoils is fun when the recipe boxes are as playful as this party's take-home favors. Scrapbooking papers, fabric daisies, and plain and patterned brads, all in showy springtime hues, add verve to these ordinary paper boxes.

Left: Put all your eggs in these delightful gingerbread baskets! For details on crafting these cookie caddies and other gingerbread containers, see page 148.

- Plain wooden Easter baskets spruced up with ribbons, bows, and name tags made from plastic frames normally used to mount 35 mm slides.

- Solid white or yellow gift bags, transformed into bunnies: (1) draw or paint a bunny face on the front of the bag; (2) glue or staple a large pair of cardstock bunny ears above the face; and (3) add a tail by gluing several cotton balls together on the back of the bag.

- Grapevine wreaths, such as those pictured on this party's cookie table (p. 28), turned into nests. Many florists carry, or can special-order, grapevine wreaths. To keep goodies from falling out the bottom, fit the inside of the wreath with a cardboard disk. Tack the disk in place using a glue gun and then conceal the disk with Easter grass.

Kataifi Birds' Nests
Makes 2 dozen (2½-inch) "nests"

Finely shredded phyllo dough, aka kataifi, makes a light and crunchy nest for candy eggs atop a cheesecake and toasted nut center. (Kataifi can be found in the frozen foods section of most specialty groceries.)

Complexity:

1

Active Time:

Type:

Hand-shaped

Prep Talk: These cookies are best enjoyed freshly baked but can be stored up to 2 days in airtight containers in the fridge. (The filling is perishable.) The kataifi will soften but can be re-crisped by placing the cookies in a 350 degree F oven for about 10 minutes. Watch carefully to avoid cracking and drying out the filling when reheating.

Cheesecake Filling
1½ (8-ounce) packages cream cheese, room temperature
6 tablespoons plus 2 teaspoons granulated sugar
2 large eggs, room temperature, beaten
¾ teaspoon finely grated lemon zest
¾ teaspoon pure vanilla extract

Kataifi "Nests"
8 ounces (½ package) kataifi (shredded phyllo dough), thawed
    according to the package instructions
¼ cup (½ stick) unsalted butter, melted
¼ cup granulated sugar
1 teaspoon ground cinnamon

¾ cups pecan halves, lightly toasted and chopped

Decoration
6 to 8 dozen small candy-coated chocolate eggs or Jordan almonds
    (3 to 4 per nest)

1. Position a rack in the center of the oven and preheat the oven to 375 degrees F. Lightly coat two standard-size (2½-inch-diameter) 12-cup muffin pans with nonstick cooking spray.

2. **Mix the Cheesecake Filling.** Place the cream cheese in the bowl of an electric mixer fitted with a paddle attachment. Beat on medium speed until smooth and creamy, less than 1 minute. Gradually add the sugar and continue to beat until it has dissolved, about 1 minute. (You should feel no grit when you smear a bit of batter between your fingers.)

   Measure out 5 tablespoons beaten egg and slowly add to the cream cheese mixture. Mix well. (Discard the remaining egg or save for another use.) To keep the batter completely smooth, scrape down the sides of the bowl regularly.

   Turn the mixer to low speed and beat in the lemon zest and

vanilla extract. Mix just until evenly combined. Set aside for use in Step 6.

3. **Prepare the kataifi for the Kataifi "Nests."** Place the kataifi in a large bowl. (Tightly wrap the leftover kataifi and refreeze for future use.) Pull apart the kataifi strands, leaving no large masses clinging together. Don't worry if the pieces break or tangle—unruly strands make for more realistic nests. Drizzle the melted butter over the top and toss to evenly coat. Combine the sugar and cinnamon in a small bowl and sprinkle the mixture over the kataifi. Toss again to uniformly coat.

4. **Form the nests.** Divide the kataifi evenly across the 24 muffin cups. Gently pat down the center of each kataifi tuft to form a 1½- to 1¾-inch depression in the middle. (The kataifi should completely line the bottom and sides of each cup.) If you don't have two muffin pans, fill the one you have and complete Steps 5 through 7; then re-use the pan once it has cooled off from its first trip to the oven. Be sure to cover any unused kataifi with plastic wrap in the meantime; otherwise, it can dry out.

5. Bake about 15 minutes, or until the kataifi is crispy and deeply browned. (The nests will shrink a bit.) Remove the pan from the oven and turn the oven down to 350 degrees F.

6. **Fill the nests and bake again.** Once the oven has reached proper temperature, sprinkle 1 scant teaspoon chopped pecans in the bottom of each nest; then top with 1 generous tablespoon cheesecake filling (or more if it fits), taking care to keep the filling off the sides of the cookies. Bake another 13 to 15 minutes, or until the filling is set and slightly puffy.

7. Immediately remove the cookies from the cups using an offset spatula to help lift them out. Transfer to wire racks and cool completely before decorating.

8. **Decorate.** Just before serving, nestle 3 to 4 candy-coated chocolate eggs (or Jordan almonds) in the top of each cookie. Serve immediately. (Refrigerating the eggs may cause their color to bleed onto the cheesecake.)

Lemon–Poppy Seed Cottontail Cookies (background) and Pink Spritz Daisy Cookies (foreground) are glued to bamboo skewers with thick Royal Icing and plunged into wheat grass after the icing has dried.

Lemon–Poppy Seed Cottontail Cookies

Makes 2 ½ to 3 dozen (2 ¼-inch) "bunny bottoms"

Here's what Peter Cottontail might look like if you were following him down the bunny trail. These amusing bunny bottoms are as tasty as they are whimsical. If time is of the essence, skip the optional decorating steps and serve the cookies un-iced. They're wonderful this way as well, particularly if you prefer your cookies less sweet.

Complexity:	Active Time:	Type:
2		Drop; hand-shaped; piped (optional "ears" and "tails")

Prep Talk: Make icing ears and tails at least 48 hours in advance of baking the cookies, and dry the glaze on the bodies at least 2 hours before applying the body parts. (*Note:* Fondant, p. 155, may also be shaped into ears as described in Step 2. In this case, let the ears dry at least a week before attaching to the cookies.) Store in airtight containers at room temperature up to 4 or 5 days.

Lemon Icing (optional)

1 recipe Royal Icing (p. 151)

1 teaspoon pure lemon extract (or ¼ teaspoon pure lemon oil, p. 156)

A few drops yellow soft gel food coloring (optional, p. 152)

About 6½ tablespoons strained freshly squeezed lemon juice, divided (optional, to thin icing)

About 2 tablespoons white nonpareils (optional, for coating the tails)

Lemon–Poppy Seed Cookies

2¼ cups plus 1 tablespoon all-purpose flour

1½ tablespoons poppy seeds

1½ teaspoons baking powder

½ teaspoon salt

¾ cup (1½ sticks) plus 3 tablespoons unsalted butter, cold, chopped into tablespoon-size pieces

¾ cup plus 2 tablespoons granulated sugar

1 large egg

1½ tablespoons finely grated lemon zest

2 tablespoons strained freshly squeezed lemon juice

1½ teaspoons pure lemon extract (or ½ to ¾ teaspoon pure lemon oil)

½ teaspoon pure vanilla extract

Powdered sugar (optional; as needed to thicken icing)

1. Make the Lemon Icing (optional). Prepare 1 recipe Royal Icing and mix in the lemon extract (or oil). If desired, add a few drops yellow food coloring to make pale yellow bunnies. Portion off about 1½ cups icing for use in Step 2. (Cover the surface of the remaining icing flush with plastic wrap and refrigerate until used in Step 7.)

2. Pipe and dry the bunny ears and tails (optional). Line two or more cookie sheets with parchment paper. Thin the icing to a thick outlining consistency (p. 152) by adding 2 to 2½ teaspoons lemon juice. Mix well. Fit a pastry bag with a small (¼-inch) round tip and fill with the icing. Pipe 2½ to 3 dozen pairs of (1½- to 2-inch-long) ears on the prepared cookie sheets. (Alternatively, make fondant ears by rolling white or tinted fondant to a ¹⁄₁₆-inch thickness with a pasta

machine or rolling pin; then cut it into ears using the top portion of a bunny-shaped cookie cutter.)

After you've shaped the ears, pipe 2½ to 3 dozen (½-inch-round) tails on a separate prepared cookie sheet. While the icing is still wet, sprinkle the white nonpareils evenly over the tails to add texture. (For details on finishing with nonpareils, aka sanding, see page 154.)

Allow the icing tails and ears to dry about 48 hours, or until easily removed from the parchment paper without breaking. (For fondant ears, allow about 1 week of drying time.) Slide a thin-bladed knife under each piece to loosen it before lifting. If the ears should break when loosening (long icing pieces can be fragile), try gently peeling the parchment paper away from them instead. First cut the parchment paper around each ear; then peel off the paper, working one ear at a time.

3. Position a rack in the center of the oven and preheat the oven to 400 degrees F. Line two or more cookie sheets with parchment paper.

4. Mix the Lemon–Poppy Seed Cookies. Combine the flour, poppy seeds, baking powder, and salt in a small bowl. Set aside.

Place the chopped butter and sugar in the bowl of an electric mixer fitted with a paddle attachment. Beat on medium-low speed until smooth, about 1 minute. Add the egg and beat until light, about 1 more minute. Scrape down the sides of the bowl as needed to ensure even mixing.

Turn the mixer to low speed and beat in the lemon zest, juice, and extracts, followed by the flour mixture. Mix just until the dry ingredients are incorporated.

5. Roll the dough between your palms into 1¼-inch balls and place about 2 inches apart on the prepared cookie sheets. For the most uniform balls, first portion the dough into mounds using a level 1½-inch (#50) scoop or 1 level tablespoon per mound; then roll into perfect balls. Flatten each ball into a 1½-inch disk by barely pressing it with the palm of your hand.

6. Bake 9 to 10 minutes, or until puffy, set, and lightly browned around

the edges. Do not overbake. Immediately transfer to wire racks with an offset spatula. Cool completely before decorating or storing.

7. Glaze the bunny bodies (optional). Remove the remaining icing from the refrigerator and bring it to room temperature. Add enough lemon juice (about 5½ tablespoons) to make a thick glaze. Mix well. (The glaze should thinly coat a "test" cookie, but you should not be able to see through it. Adjust the glaze consistency as needed by adding more juice to thin it or powdered sugar to thicken it.)

Set a wire rack over a sheet of parchment paper. (The paper will catch the glaze drippings and make for easier cleanup later.) Work with one cookie at a time. Hold the cookie by the bottom and completely immerse its top in the glaze. Turn the cookie right side up and gently shake it to remove excess glaze and to smooth the top. Place on the rack. Repeat with the remaining cookies.

Before the glaze dries, slide a paring knife under each cookie to sever any drippings that may be clinging to the rack. (The glaze will otherwise dry onto the rack, making it more difficult to remove the cookies later.) Dry at least 2 hours before assembling.

8. Assemble the bunnies (optional). Portion off about ½ cup of the remaining glaze and add enough powdered sugar to make a thick paste for gluing. Fill a parchment pastry cone with the icing and cut a small (⅛-inch) hole in the tip.

Work with one cookie at a time. Glue a tail to the top of the cookie near an edge; then glue one pair of ears to the back of the cookie. The ears should extend 1½ to 2 inches off the edge opposite the tail. Set the cookie aside and do not move it until the ears have dried in place. Repeat with the remaining cookies. Store as directed. Do not stack the cookies, or the ears may break.

Note: There will be leftover Royal Icing. Cover and store as directed (p. 151) for another use.

Pink Spritz Daisy Cookies
Makes 8½ to 9 dozen (1¾- to 2-inch) cookies

This book wouldn't be complete without a tribute to the famous pink daisy cookie enjoyed at my first cookie swap.

Complexity:	Active Time:	Type:
①		Pressed

Prep Talk: Store in airtight containers at room temperature up to 2 weeks.

2¼ cups all-purpose flour
½ teaspoon salt
4 ounces almond paste, room temperature
½ cup plus 2 tablespoons granulated sugar
½ cup (1 stick) unsalted butter, slightly softened
½ cup (½ stick) butter-flavored shortening
1 large egg
1½ teaspoons pure almond extract, or to taste
½ teaspoon pure vanilla extract
About 11 to 12 drops pink soft gel food coloring (optional, p. 152)

Decoration (optional)
½ cup Royal Icing (p. 151), thinned for beadwork (p. 152)
¼ teaspoon pure almond extract, or to taste
About 6 drops yellow soft gel food coloring, or to desired shade

1. Position a rack in the center of the oven and preheat the oven to 400 degrees F. Set aside two or more unlined and ungreased cookie sheets for later use. (Cookies pressed at a 90-degree angle to the pan, such as these daisies, will adhere better to an unprepared cookie sheet.)

2. Combine the flour and salt in a small bowl. Set aside for use in Step 5.

3. Place the almond paste in the bowl of a food processor fitted with

a metal blade and process to a very fine meal. Set aside for use in Step 4.

4. Place the sugar, butter, and shortening in the bowl of an electric mixer fitted with a paddle attachment and beat on medium speed until creamy. (*Note:* To minimize spreading of the cookies, the butter should be slightly softened—that is, pliable but not squishy.) Add the almond paste, followed by the egg and extracts, and beat 1 to 2 minutes longer, or until light and fluffy. Beat in the food coloring, if desired, to tint the dough bright pink. Mix until the color is evenly distributed.

5. Turn the mixer to low speed and gradually add the dry ingredients, mixing just until combined. Stir as needed to bring the dough completely together. There should be no dry spots.

6. Fill a cookie press with the dough and fit the end of the press with a daisy-shaped disk. Hold the press at a 90-degree angle to the cookie sheet and press out daisy shapes, spacing them about 1 inch apart.

7. Bake 6 to 7 minutes, or until very lightly browned around the edges. (The cookies should show minimal discoloration.) Carefully transfer to wire racks with an offset spatula and cool completely before decorating or storing.

8. Decorate (optional). Flavor ½ cup Royal Icing, thinned to the consistency for beadwork (p. 152), with the almond extract. For a bright yellow color, add about 6 drops yellow food coloring and mix well. Fill a parchment pastry cone with the icing and cut a small (⅛- to ¼-inch) hole in the tip. Pipe a large bead in the center of each cookie. Let the icing dry before serving or storing as directed above.

   Note: There will be a small amount of leftover Royal Icing. Cover and store as directed (p. 151) for another use.

Bunny Trail Mix Cookies

Makes about 3 dozen (2 ¼- to 2 ½-inch) cookies

Granola, raisins, and candy-coated chocolate bits . . . yes, everything the Easter Bunny might want for sustenance on the trail is in this super-stuffed, quick-mix cookie.

Complexity:

Active Time:

Type:

Drop; hand-shaped

Prep Talk: Store in airtight containers at room temperature up to 1 week.

1½ cups plus 2 tablespoons all-purpose flour

¾ teaspoon cream of tartar

¾ teaspoon baking soda

¼ teaspoon salt

½ cup plus 3 tablespoons granulated sugar

¼ cup (½ stick) plus 1 tablespoon unsalted butter, softened

¼ cup (¼ stick) butter-flavored shortening

1 large egg

2 teaspoons finely grated orange zest

1 teaspoon pure vanilla extract

1 cup granola cereal (preferably sweetened, without raisins or other mix-ins)

¾ cup raisins

½ cup candy-coated chocolate bits

Additional candy-coated chocolate bits (optional, for pressing into cookie tops)

1. Position a rack in the center of the oven and preheat the oven to 375 degrees F. Line two or more cookie sheets with parchment paper.

2. Combine the flour, cream of tartar, baking soda, and salt in a small bowl. Set aside for use in Step 4.

3. Place the sugar, butter, and shortening in the bowl of an electric mixer fitted with a paddle attachment. Beat on medium speed until creamy. Add the egg and beat until light and fluffy, about 1 to 2 minutes. Scrape down the sides of the bowl as needed to ensure even mixing.

4. Turn the mixer to low speed and add the orange zest and vanilla extract, followed by the flour mixture. Mix just until the dry ingredients are evenly incorporated.

5. Stir in the granola, raisins, and chocolate bits.

6. Roll the dough between your palms into 1-inch balls and place about 2 inches apart on the prepared cookie sheets. For the most uniform balls, first portion the dough into 1-inch mounds using a slightly rounded 1⅜-inch (#70) scoop or about 2 level teaspoons per mound; then roll into perfect balls. Flatten the cookies into 1½-inch disks by gently pressing them with the palm of your hand.

7. Bake 8 to 9 minutes, or until lightly browned. (If you want to see more spring-y color on top, stud the cookies with additional chocolate bits about midway through baking.) Immediately transfer the cookies to wire racks, using an offset spatula to prevent breakage. Cool completely before storing.

Shortbread Easter Bonnets

Makes about 2 ½ dozen (2 ½ x ½-inch-tall) "bonnets"
Iced and double-decked, buttery cardamom shortbread rounds are transformed into fancy Easter hats. Add dainty fondant ribbons and flowers, or, to save time, pipe a single Royal Icing band around the crown of each hat.

Complexity:
②

Active Time:

Type:
Rolled

Prep Talk: The dough must be chilled 1 to 2 hours before rolling and cutting. The dough can be frozen up to 1 month with minimal loss of flavor if wrapped tightly in plastic and then foil. Store baked cookies in airtight containers at room temperature no longer than 2 weeks.

Cardamom Shortbread

1 recipe Shortbread, Straight Up (p. 143), powdered sugar and sugar
    for sprinkling omitted
1 teaspoon ground cardamom
¼ cup firmly packed light brown sugar
½ teaspoon pure vanilla extract

Lemon Royal Icing

½ recipe Royal Icing (p. 151), thinned for top-coating (p. 152)
⅜ teaspoon pure lemon extract, or to taste
Soft gel food coloring of your choice, to desired shade (optional, p. 152)

Decoration (optional, see "Fun with Fondant," p. 155)

About 2 ½ dozen (¼ x 5-inch) fondant bands (for wrapping around
    bonnet brims, 1 per cookie)
About 2 ½ dozen tiny (¼-inch) fondant daisies (1 per cookie)
About 5 dozen tiny (¼-inch) fondant leaves (2 per cookie)

1. **Mix the Cardamom Shortbread.** Prepare 1 recipe Shortbread, Straight Up, adding the cardamom to the flour mixture at the end of Step 1 (p. 143). Replace the powdered sugar with the brown sugar and increase the vanilla extract by ½ teaspoon in Step 2. Chill the dough and preheat the oven as directed.

2. On a lightly floured surface, roll the dough to a ³⁄₁₆-inch thickness and cut out about 2 ½ dozen rounds with a fluted 2 ½-inch round cookie cutter. Place the rounds 1 inch apart on parchment paper–lined cookie sheets. Re-roll the remaining dough to a ³⁄₈-inch thickness and cut out about 2 ½ dozen small rounds using a straight-edged 1¼-inch round cookie cutter. Place these cookies on a separate parchment paper–lined cookie sheet. Do not sprinkle the cookie tops with sugar as instructed in Shortbread, Straight Up, as the sugar will make it more difficult to top-coat the cookies in Step 5.

3. Bake the large thin rounds for 17 to 20 minutes, or until lightly browned around the edges. Bake the small thick rounds closer to 20 to 23 minutes. Rotate the cookie sheets as needed to ensure even browning. Cool as directed.

4. **Mix the Lemon Royal Icing.** Prepare ½ recipe Royal Icing, thinned for top-coating (p. 152). Add the lemon extract and food coloring, if desired. Mix well.

5. **Top-coat the cookies.** Work with one cookie at a time. Using the handle-end of a clean craft paintbrush (about ¼-inch diameter), apply a small amount of icing to the top center of the cookie. Working quickly before the icing sets, spread the icing across the cookie top with the tip of the handle. Repeat with the remaining cookies. (You may also add beadwork borders or outlines if desired. See page 152 for decorating techniques.) Set aside to dry at least 3 hours.

6. **Assemble the bonnets.** Double-deck a large cookie and a small cookie, placing the larger one on the bottom. Secure the cookies to one another with a dab of leftover icing. Repeat until all of the cookies have been stacked into bonnets. Allow the icing to set 20 to 30 minutes before further decorating.

7. **Decorate (optional).** Fill a parchment paper pastry cone with leftover icing and cut a small (less than ⅛-inch) hole in the tip. Use the icing to glue a small fondant band around the crown of each bonnet and a fondant daisy and two leaves at the point where the ends meet. Allow the icing to set before moving. Store as directed above.

Quick Cutout Marshmallow Peeps (and Bunnies)

Makes about 2 ½ dozen (1¾ x 2 ½-inch) "chicks," or about 1½ dozen (1¾ x 3¼-inch) "bunnies"

Okay, so these marshmallow treats aren't cookies, but they do require cookie cutters. They also look extra sweet embellished with any number of cookie decorating techniques. *Note:* While the making of the sugar syrup in Step 2 requires adult supervision, this recipe is otherwise a great project for kids. Shaping peeps is far easier with a cookie cutter than with the oft-required pastry bag.

Complexity:

1

Active Time:

Type:

N/A

Prep Talk: Though not essential, a candy thermometer is helpful in Step 2. The marshmallow must dry at least 4 hours at room temperature before cutting. Store in airtight containers at room temperature for 2 to 3 weeks.

About 1⅓ cups pale yellow, fine-grained sanding sugar, divided (for dusting the pan and chicks)
1 cup cold water, divided
2 cups granulated sugar

¾ cup light corn syrup

½ teaspoon salt

3 envelopes (about 2¼ teaspoons each) unflavored gelatin

1½ teaspoons finely grated lemon zest

1 tablespoon strained freshly squeezed lemon juice

½ teaspoon pure lemon extract

5 or more drops yellow soft gel food coloring, to desired shade
(optional, p. 152)

Decoration (optional)

½ recipe Royal Icing (p. 151), thinned for beadwork (p. 152)

Soft gel food coloring in colors of your choice

1½ to 2½ dozen tiny (¼-inch) fondant daisies or other
embellishments (1 per cookie, p. 155)

1. Generously coat the bottom and sides of a 10 x 15 x 1-inch jelly-roll pan with nonstick cooking spray. Line the bottom of the pan with parchment paper and lightly coat the paper with more cooking spray. Sprinkle about ⅔ cup sanding sugar over the pan so that it coats the sides and covers the bottom in a thick, even layer. (You should not see through the sugar to the bottom of the pan.) Gently shake the pan to evenly distribute any loose sugar, but do not shake out the excess sugar.

2. Combine ½ cup water, the granulated sugar, corn syrup, and salt in a medium (3-quart) saucepan and set over medium-high heat. Bring the mixture to a boil, stirring as needed until the sugar has dissolved. Cover for a few minutes to allow any sugar crystals on the side of the pan to dissolve. Uncover and continue to boil, without stirring, until the syrup registers 238 to 240 degrees F on a candy thermometer. (Alternatively, when ready, a drop of syrup will form a soft, malleable ball when placed in a cup of ice water.)

3. While the syrup is boiling in Step 2, pour the remaining water into the bowl of an electric mixer fitted with a whip attachment. Slowly sprinkle the gelatin over the top, waiting for one envelope of gelatin to be completely absorbed by the water before sprinkling the next. Allow the gelatin to sit until it is thoroughly moistened. (If a few dry spots remain on top, leave them be. Do not stir, or the gelatin will get lumpy.)

4. Add a few tablespoons of the hot sugar syrup to the gelatin mixture to begin to dissolve it. Turn the mixer to medium speed and add the remaining hot sugar syrup in a slow, steady stream. When all of the sugar syrup has been incorporated, quickly scrape down the sides of the bowl.

5. Turn the mixer to high speed and beat until the mixture is thick, glossy, and very white, about 10 minutes. (You will hear the cadence of your mixer change as the meringue approaches the proper thickness. The meringue will also cling in a large mass to the beater when it is ready.) Add the lemon zest, juice, extract, and food coloring, if desired, in the last few minutes of beating. *Note:* The yellow sanding sugar will completely coat the marshmallow cutouts, so they will appear yellow from the outside even if the marshmallow isn't tinted.

6. Immediately turn the mixture into the prepared pan and level with a small offset spatula. Sprinkle the remaining sanding sugar evenly over the top, completely covering the marshmallow. Let dry uncovered at room temperature at least 4 hours. Avoid drying longer than 12 hours, as the marshmallow top can become tough and difficult to cut.

7. Cut out the chicks (or bunnies). Run a paring knife along the edge of the pan to loosen any stuck marshmallow, and invert the pan onto a clean work surface. (The bottom of the marshmallow will be smoother than the top, and is, therefore, the better side to "face forward.") Reserve any loose sanding sugar that spills off of the marshmallow.

   Lightly coat a small (about 1¾ x 2½- to 3¼-inch) chick or bunny cookie cutter with nonstick cooking spray. (*Note:* You will need a cutter that is at least 1 inch deep in order to cut through the marshmallow without squishing it.) Cut out chicks (or bunnies) until all the marshmallow is used. To prevent sticking, clean and grease the cutter between cuts as needed. If desired, roll the cutouts in the reserved sanding sugar to cover the sides. Shake off any excess sugar and set the cutouts aside on parchment paper–lined cookie sheets, or store if you don't plan to decorate them immediately.

8. Decorate (optional). Tint ½ recipe Royal Icing, thinned for beadwork, with food coloring, and pipe on "eyes," "tails," and other details using the beadwork technique (p. 153). Add fondant daisies or other embellishments as desired.

Cocoa-Mint Sandwiches

Lemon-Thyme Bonbons

NOT YOUR GARDEN-VARIETY GARDEN PARTY

With April showers finally past, May beckons us to throw open our doors and to rejoice in the start of the outdoor party season. And what more fitting celebration than this teatime cookie swap? Set in the garden and blooming with references to flowers and herbs, it looks and tastes as if it is the handiwork of Mother Nature.

The party theme is planted with the save-the-date cards, replicas of old-time seed packs. Closer to the party, gingerbread May Day baskets are left dangling on guests' doors. Filled with fresh-picked blossoms and specifics of the upcoming fête, these edible invitations both enchant and inform.

At the front gate, a garden pot overgrown with gingerbread roses welcomes party-goers. Uncommon herb and flower-scented cookies appear down the path, set on pots and planters rooted in a moss-covered tabletop. Shaped mostly into dainty petits fours, these treats allow guests to sample guilt-free. The perfect indulgence for an elegant tea!

The pleasure continues even as the afternoon sun fades. Contented guests file the party recipes into empty seed packets and wind their way back along the path. As the gate closes, the hostess bids farewell with leftover cookies arranged in lovely fabric-covered flower pots.

Cause to Celebrate:
May Day; Mothers' Day; a springtime birthday; the much anticipated end of a long winter; Earth Day; a gathering of good friends for refreshment and renewal; a bridal shower; a celebration of new beginnings—a baby, a career change, a first home!

Clockwise from the teacup caddy at top: Mixed Seed Wafers, Lavender Shortbread (among decorated sugar cookies), Rosemary Blonde Brownies, Anise-Scented Springerle, Cocoa-Mint Sandwich Cookies, and Lemon-Thyme Bonbons (center). Not pictured: Rosewater Marguerites.

Tip guests off at the start by sending invitations that draw attention to the garden theme. Inside these May Day baskets crafted from gingerbread are paper scrolls containing the party information and charming garden images reproduced from vintage almanacs. See "How to Make Gingerbread Boxes and Baskets" (p. 148) for more details.

Stand-ins *(top left)*
Quick paper greetings . . .

If time doesn't allow for gingerbread May Day baskets, try simpler paper alternatives, such as these "Forget-Me-Not" save-the-date cards fashioned into seed packets and invitations resembling the *Farmers' Almanac.*

To make the save-the-date packets: Digitally scan the front and back of real seed packets. Use photo-editing software to superimpose the party information along with photos of the honored guests. Print both sides onto paper or cardstock and cut them out, leaving about ¼ inch extra along the sides and bottom of each scanned image. Score around each image. Fold back the extra paper along the scored lines toward the unprinted side of the paper. Apply glue to the tops of these folded "flaps" and place the two pieces of the packet back to back. Gently press along the sides and bottom to seal; then press the packet flat between books or other heavy objects for a few hours. Fill with seeds and seal the opening at the top with more glue before mailing.

Everything's Coming up Roses
To "plant" rose, bird, and birdhouse cookies: Start with a pot filled with ivy or other greenery. Glue the cookies to ¼-inch dowel rods with thick Royal Icing and let the icing dry completely before plunging the rods into the potting soil.

Top left: Gussy up papier-mâché garden pots (p. 156) with vintage floral fabrics, scrapbooking paper, and garden twine (pictured along the upper edges of the pots), and fill with surplus cookies for guests to take home. As an extra touch, personalize the pots with "garden stakes" decorated with images and/or names of your guests.

Bottom left: Edible wafer papers—thin, translucent sheets of dehydrated potato starch, water, and vegetable oil—are a great vehicle for quickly transferring lavish detail to cookies. Wafer papers come pre-printed with food-safe dyes in a variety of patterns, such as the pink toile design shown here and on the baskets on page 48. For wafer paper techniques, see page 154; for sources of wafer paper and sugarcoated roses (pictured on the cookie tops), see page 156.

Top right: A bed of sheet moss and rosebuds is an effortless alternative to expensive linens. *Note:* Your local florist may not have sheet moss on hand, so be sure to order in advance.

Bottom right: For these garden-themed favors, either empty out real seed packets after neatly cutting off the tops or proceed as you would to make save-the-date packets (p. 49) but replace the seeds with recipe cards.

Rosemary Blonde Brownies

Makes about 4 dozen (1½-inch) squares or 4½ dozen
(1¼ x 1½-inch) ovals

To morph these simple bars into stylish petits fours, cut the cookie
block into small ovals or rounds and pipe florets of Rosemary Ganache
(p. 53) or Italian Buttercream (p. 150) on top. *Note:* For kids, omit the
rosemary in both the brownie and the ganache topping and boost the
quantity of chocolate chips and other mix-ins to taste.

Complexity: Active Time: Type:

1   Bar

Prep Talk: Cool the bars completely (about 2 hours) before topping
with ganache. Decorated bars should be stored in the refrigerator.
(The topping is perishable.) If the brownies have not been decorated, they are better stored at room temperature. Bars will stay

2½ cups all-purpose flour

2½ tablespoons chopped fresh rosemary leaves
    (4 to 5 rosemary sprigs, stems removed)

2 teaspoons baking powder

³⁄₈ teaspoon salt

1¼ cups (2½ sticks) unsalted butter, chopped into
    tablespoon-size pieces

2¼ cups firmly packed light brown sugar

3 large eggs, room temperature

2 teaspoons pure vanilla extract

1½ cups pecan halves, toasted, cooled, and coarsely chopped

1 cup premium milk or semisweet chocolate chips

Rosemary Ganache (optional)

¾ recipe Ganache (p. 149)

¼ cup loosely packed fresh rosemary leaves, coarsely chopped
    (4 to 5 sprigs, stems removed)

Decoration (optional)

About 4 dozen small (½-inch) rosemary sprigs (1 per brownie)

1. Position a rack in the center of the oven and preheat the oven to 350 degrees F. Line a 10 x 15 x 1-inch jelly-roll pan with foil, leaving a 1-inch overhang around the top edge of the pan. Smooth out any big wrinkles in the foil and then lightly coat with nonstick cooking spray.

2. Combine the flour, rosemary, baking powder, and salt together in the bowl of a food processor fitted with a metal blade. Process until the rosemary is reduced to very small pieces. (*Note:* If the rosemary isn't chopped before going into the processor, it will be harder to finely grind.) Set aside for use in Step 4.

3. Place the butter in a medium (3-quart) saucepan over low heat. Once the butter has fully melted, remove it from the heat and stir in the brown sugar, mixing until smooth. (*Note:* Don't be surprised if the butter and sugar do not completely come together at this point; some separation is normal.) Cool a few minutes and then add the eggs one at a time, whisking well after each addition.

4. Stir in the vanilla extract. Gradually add the flour mixture, whisking all the while to keep the batter lump-free. Cool before stirring in the pecans and chocolate chips. (Otherwise, the chips will melt.) Spoon the batter evenly into the prepared pan and level with a small offset spatula. (The batter will be less than 1 inch thick, but it will rise to the top of the pan.)

5. Bake until a cake tester inserted into the center comes out with moist crumbs on it and the brownie is just starting to pull away from the edges of the pan, about 22 to 24 minutes. Transfer to a wire rack and cool completely in the pan.

6. Remove the brownies from the pan in one block by gently pulling up on the foil overhang. Place directly on a cutting board. Remove all foil and trim any uneven edges before cutting into 1½-inch squares (or ovals).

7. Make the Rosemary Ganache (optional). This topping will set if made too far in advance, so make it no sooner than you intend to decorate the cookies. Prepare ¾ recipe Ganache, following the instructions on pages 149 and 150, but add the rosemary to the scalded cream in Step 2. Let the herbs steep in the warm cream about 30 minutes. Reheat the cream to the scalding point before proceeding to Step 3. (*Note:* The rosemary will be strained out in this step.) Chill as directed in Step 4 for piping ganache.

8. Decorate (optional). Fit a pastry bag with a medium (³⁄₈-inch) 6- to 8-pronged star tip and fill with the ganache. Pipe a small floret of icing on top of each brownie and garnish with a sprig of rosemary, if desired. Serve immediately or store as directed.

Cocoa-Mint Sandwich Cookies (right teacup) and Lemon-Thyme Bonbons (left teacup)

Cocoa-Mint Sandwich Cookies
Makes about 4 ½ dozen (1½-inch) sandwiches

Though refreshingly cool with a white chocolate–mint filling, these sandwiches generate warm feelings when shared among friends.

Complexity:

Active Time:

Type:
Rolled; sandwich

Prep Talk: Both the filling and dough require chilling before they can be used—about 20 minutes for the former and at least 1½ to 2 hours for the latter. The dough can be frozen up to 1 month with minimal loss of flavor if tightly wrapped in plastic and then foil. Store baked unfilled cookies up to 1 week in airtight containers at room temperature. Once filled, the cookies are best served immediately. Otherwise, refrigerate (the filling is perishable) and serve within 1 to 2 days, before the cocoa wafers soften in the fridge.

Cocoa Wafer Dough

2 cups sifted all-purpose flour

½ cup unsweetened Dutch-process cocoa powder

³/₈ teaspoon salt

1 cup (2 sticks) unsalted butter, softened

¾ cup plus 4 tablespoons granulated sugar, divided

2 large eggs, room temperature

1 teaspoon pure mint extract

About 4 ounces premium semisweet chocolate, melted (for coating)

White Chocolate–Mint Filling

1 recipe Ganache, White Chocolate Variation (p. 150), cream increased to 1 cup

⅓ cup loosely packed fresh mint leaves (less than half of a ²/₃-ounce package, stems removed), or to taste

¼ teaspoon pure mint extract

1. Mix the Cocoa Wafer Dough. Combine the flour, cocoa powder, and salt in a small bowl and set aside.

   Place the butter and ¾ cup sugar in the bowl of an electric mixer fitted with a paddle attachment. Beat on medium speed until creamy, about 1 minute. Add the eggs one at a time, beating well after each addition. Scrape down the sides of the bowl as needed to ensure even mixing. Continue to beat until light and fluffy, about 1 more minute.

   Turn the mixer to low speed and add the mint extract. Gradually add the flour mixture, blending just until evenly incorporated.

2. Divide the dough into two equal portions and flatten each portion into a disk. Wrap each disk tightly in plastic and refrigerate at least 1½ to 2 hours, or until firm enough to roll.

3. Position a rack in the center of the oven and preheat the oven to 350 degrees F. Line two or more cookie sheets with parchment paper.

4. Work with one disk of dough at a time. On a lightly floured work surface, roll the dough to a ⅛-inch thickness. Dust the work surface and rolling pin with additional flour as needed to keep the dough from sticking. (This dough is softer than that used for some of the other rolled cookies in this book, so it may require more dusting.) Cut out small disks using a fluted 1½-inch round cookie cutter. (Periodically clean off the cutter and dust it with flour to prevent sticking.) Transfer the cutouts to the prepared cookie sheets, spacing them about 1 inch apart. Dust off any excess flour on the cookie tops with a pastry brush. Repeat with the remaining dough. For best results, briefly chill the dough scraps before re-rolling.

5. Sprinkle the cookie tops generously with the remaining sugar (about 1 tablespoon sugar per cookie sheet) and bake 14 to 16 minutes, or until very firm. Immediately transfer to wire racks and cool completely before coating with chocolate and filling.

6. Using a small knife or offset spatula, spread a thin layer of melted semisweet chocolate on the back of each cookie. Place the cookies on parchment paper–lined cookie sheets, chocolate side up, and set in the refrigerator about 10 minutes or until the chocolate is set.

7. Prepare the White Chocolate–Mint Filling. This filling will set if made too far in advance, so make it no sooner than you intend to fill the cookies. Prepare 1 recipe Ganache, White Chocolate Variation, as directed on page 150, except increase the cream to 1 cup. Coarsely chop or tear the mint and place it in the scalded cream at the end of Step 2. Allow the mint to steep in the warm cream about 30 minutes; then reheat the cream to the scalding point before proceeding to Step 3. (*Note:* The mint will be strained out in this step.) Stir in the mint extract at the end.

   Chill as directed in Step 4 (p. 150) for piping ganache, about 20 minutes or until slightly thickened. Transfer to the bowl of an electric mixer fitted with a whip attachment. Beat on medium speed just until the ganache turns a shade whiter and holds the "tracks" left by the beater. Do not overbeat, or the ganache will break and become grainy.

8. Assemble the sandwiches. Work quickly before the ganache sets. Fit a pastry bag with a medium (⅜-inch) round tip and fill the bag with the ganache. Pipe a small (about 1¼-inch-diameter) mound of filling on the chocolate-coated side of half of the cookies. Top each mound with another cookie, placed chocolate side down. Press gently to squeeze the ganache to the edges. Serve immediately or store as directed. *Note:* There will be some leftover filling. Try it gently heated and spooned over ice cream.

Lemon-Thyme Bonbons
Makes 5 to 5 ½ dozen (1¾-inch) "bonbons"

Both filled and frosted, this bite-size cookie is indulgent without being excessive. *Note:* For a more kid-friendly version, omit the thyme and substitute peach or apricot jam for the lemon marmalade.

Complexity:	Active Time:	Type:
❷		Rolled; sandwich

Prep Talk: The dough must be chilled 2½ to 3 hours before rolling and cutting. The dough can be frozen up to 1 month with minimal loss of flavor if tightly wrapped in plastic and then foil. Store baked cookies in airtight containers at room temperature up to 3 to 4 days. For the crunchiest texture, enjoy immediately, as the cookies soften after 1 day.

Lemon-Cream Cheese Dough

2 cups all-purpose flour

½ teaspoon baking powder

½ teaspoon salt

⅛ teaspoon baking soda

⅔ cup (1 stick plus 2⅔ tablespoons) unsalted butter, softened

1 (3-ounce) package cream cheese, room temperature

¾ cup granulated sugar

1 large egg

2 teaspoons finely grated lemon zest

1 teaspoon strained freshly squeezed lemon juice

Marmalade-Thyme Filling

¾ cup plus 2 tablespoons lemon marmalade, or peach or apricot jam

8 to 10 sprigs fresh garden or lemon thyme

Additional fresh garden or lemon thyme leaves, to taste (for sprinkling)

Decoration (optional)

½ recipe Royal Icing (p. 151), thinned for top-coating or outlining (see Step 7; also p. 152)

⅜ teaspoon pure lemon extract, or to taste

A few drops soft gel food coloring of your choice (p. 152)

1. **Mix the Lemon-Cream Cheese Dough.** Combine the flour, baking powder, salt, and baking soda in a small bowl and set aside.

    Place the butter and cream cheese in the bowl of an electric mixer fitted with a paddle attachment. Beat on medium speed until creamy. Gradually add the sugar, followed by the egg, and beat until light and fluffy, about 1 minute. Turn the mixer to low speed and beat in the lemon zest and juice.

    Gradually add the flour mixture, mixing just until combined.

2. Divide the dough into four equal portions and flatten each portion into a disk. Wrap each disk tightly in plastic and refrigerate 2½ to 3 hours, or until firm enough to roll without sticking.

3. **Make the Marmalade-Thyme Filling.** While the dough is chilling, place the marmalade (or jam) in a small nonreactive (stainless steel or coated) saucepan over medium heat. Break up any large

(½-inch-plus) pieces of fruit and heat the marmalade until loose and bubbly. Add the thyme sprigs and cook another 1 to 2 minutes over low heat. Let the filling cool to room temperature and remove the thyme sprigs.

4. Position a rack in the middle of the oven and preheat the oven to 350 degrees F. Line two or more cookie sheets with parchment paper.

5. Work with one disk of dough at a time. On a lightly floured work surface, roll the dough to a ⅛-inch thickness. Cut out about 30 small disks using a 1½-inch round cookie cutter. (If needed, briefly chill the dough scraps before re-rolling.) Place half of the disks on the prepared cookie sheets, spacing them about 1 inch apart. Spoon a level ½ teaspoon marmalade filling onto the top center of each disk, taking care to keep the filling away from the cookie edges. (Do not spread the filling. Leaving it in a mound will lead to rounder, puffier bonbons.) Sprinkle fresh thyme leaves evenly over the filling, if desired; then cover each cookie with one of the reserved disks. Gently press the edges of the disks together to seal in the filling. Repeat with the remaining dough.

6. Bake 12 to 14 minutes, or until lightly browned on the bottom. Immediately transfer to wire racks with an offset spatula and cool completely before decorating or storing.

7. Decorate (optional). Prepare ½ recipe Royal Icing and flavor with the lemon extract. For a textured finish, such as the icing swirls on the bonbons (pictured, p. 54), thin the icing to outlining consistency as instructed on page 152. For a smoother, flatter finish, the icing must be thinned further to top-coating consistency (p. 152.) Portion the icing into smaller quantities and tint each portion to a soft pastel shade using food coloring of your choice. Spread a small amount of icing (about ½ teaspoon) on top of each cookie. (I like to apply and spread the icing with the handle-end of a small craft paintbrush, just as I apply Royal Icing when top-coating sugar cookies. To make swirls, simply move the end of the paintbrush in small circles.) Let the icing dry before serving or storing.

    Note: There will be leftover Royal Icing. Cover and store as directed (p. 151) for another use.

Lavender Shortbread

Makes 3 to 3½ dozen (1¾ x 2¼-inch) oval cookies

Bake this recipe, and you'll see why lavender has come to mean "loyalty." This cookie's fragrant bouquet and buttery texture invariably attract a devoted following.

Complexity:	Active Time:	Type:
1		Rolled

Prep Talk: The dough must be chilled 1 to 2 hours before rolling and cutting. The dough can be frozen up to 1 month with minimal loss of flavor if wrapped tightly in plastic and then foil. Store baked cookies in airtight containers at room temperature no longer than 2 weeks.

1 recipe Shortbread, Straight Up (p. 143)
2 tablespoons dried lavender flowers (p. 156), or to taste

Decoration (optional)
About ⅓ cup gold or pastel nonpareils
About ½ cup Royal Icing (p. 151)

1. Follow the directions for Shortbread, Straight Up, except combine the lavender flowers with the almonds in Step 1 (p. 143). Process until the lavender is very finely ground.

2. Roll the dough as instructed in Step 5 (p. 143), but cut it into small rounds or ovals. (For tea-party-size portions, I like to use a 1¾ x 2¼-inch oval cutter.)

3. Bake closer to 25 minutes rather than the 25 to 30 minutes indicated for larger cookies. Cool completely before decorating or storing.

4. Decorate (optional). Pour the nonpareils into a small cake pan or bowl to form a shallow layer. Fill a parchment pastry cone with Royal Icing and cut a small (⅛-inch) hole in the tip. Work with one cookie at a time. Pipe a thin border of icing around the cookie edge. Immediately dip the cookie in the nonpareils to cover the icing. Dry before serving.

Mixed Seed Wafers

Makes 3½ to 4 dozen (2 ¼- to 2 ½-inch) wafers

An enticing dichotomy, this cookie is thin and crisp, yet it's packed with the robust flavor you'd expect of a bulkier cookie.

Complexity:

Active Time:

Type: Drop; hand-shaped

Prep Talk: Silicone baking mats are recommended for this recipe, though nonstick cookie sheets can be substituted (see Step 4, below). Store the wafers in airtight containers at room temperature up to 2 weeks. Contain them as soon as they've cooled. Due to their high sugar content, they will quickly attract moisture and get soft if not properly stored.

¼ cup plus 2 tablespoons all-purpose flour

¼ cup plus 1 tablespoon flax seed, lightly toasted and cooled (available in the bulk foods sections of most health and organic food stores)

1½ tablespoons caraway seed, lightly toasted and cooled

¼ teaspoon baking soda

⅛ teaspoon salt

¼ cup (½ stick) plus 2 tablespoons unsalted butter, cut into tablespoon-size pieces

¾ cup firmly packed dark brown sugar

1 large egg, beaten

¾ teaspoon pure vanilla extract

1. Combine the flour, flax seed, caraway seed, baking soda, and salt in a small bowl and set aside for use in Step 3.

2. Place the butter in a medium (3-quart) saucepan and melt over medium heat. Remove from the heat and immediately add the brown sugar, stirring until it is uniformly moistened. Cool to lukewarm. *Note:* Some separation of the butter from the sugar may occur, but this is not a problem.

3. Measure out 1½ tablespoons beaten egg and whisk into the butter mixture along with the vanilla extract. (Discard the remaining egg or save for another use.) Gradually add the flour mixture, stirring until evenly incorporated. The dough will be quite loose. Cool 25 to 30 minutes, or until the dough can be rolled into balls that hold their shape without much spreading. (You can bake the cookies immediately, but they will bake into more uniform rounds if you let the dough cool first. Transferring the dough to a bowl will expedite the cooling process.)

4. Position a rack in the center of the oven and preheat the oven to 325 degrees F. Line two or more cookie sheets with silicone baking mats. You can also use nonstick cookie sheets, though the cookies will bake more quickly on them, especially if they are dark. A dark pan can also make it more difficult to determine when the cookies are properly browned. (*Note:* With nonstick cookie sheets, no pan preparation is necessary. The cookies tend to misshape on parchment paper and will get doughy if baked on greased and floured pans.)

5. Portion the dough into small mounds using a level 1- to 1⅛-inch (#100) scoop or 1 level teaspoon per mound. Drop the mounds directly onto the prepared (or nonstick) cookie sheets, spacing them 2 to 2½ inches apart. Roll the mounds between your palms to form uniform ¾-inch balls and set the balls back on the cookie sheets.

6. Bake 11 to 12 minutes, or until the balls have flattened and turned a rich golden brown through to the center. Rotate the cookie sheets as needed to ensure even browning. Watch carefully toward the end of the baking process, as the wafers can quickly go from done to burned.

7. Cool the wafers 2 to 3 minutes on the cookie sheets, or until the wafers are stiff enough to lift with an offset spatula without tearing. (Do not cool any longer on nonstick cookie sheets, or, ironically, the wafers will stick.) Cool completely before storing. *Note:* If the wafers do not turn completely crisp as they cool, they are underbaked. Return them to the oven for a few more minutes and test their crispness again.

Anise-Scented Springerle

Makes 4 ½ to 5 dozen (2 ¼-inch) round cookies

Springerle, beautifully embossed cookies of German descent, are most often associated with Christmas. However, with the wealth of stunning molds and rolling pins (used to imprint) now available online (p. 156), there's no reason these pillow-y cookies can't be enjoyed any time. Molds carved with roses and birds make the perfect statement here. *Note:* Don't rush the drying time in Step 12. Exposing the unbaked cookies to air "sets" the embossed pattern so that it stays well defined in the heat of the oven.

Complexity:

Active Time:

Type:

Rolled (and embossed)

Prep Talk: The dough must be refrigerated about 1 hour before rolling and embossing, and then air-dried at least 8 to 10 hours before baking. Generally, the longer the drying time, the sharper the final impression. These cookies keep 1 to 2 months in airtight containers at room temperature. If you prefer a softer texture, eat within 1 week. The cookies will harden over time and eventually require dunking, but they will also take on a stronger anise flavor, especially if you toss extra seeds into the storage container.

About 5 to 5 ¼ cups sifted cake flour, divided

2 teaspoons baking powder

¼ teaspoon salt

4 large eggs

2 ½ cups sifted powdered sugar

1 cup sifted superfine sugar

1 tablespoon finely grated lemon zest

½ teaspoon pure anise extract

3 tablespoons unsalted butter, melted

2 ½ to 3 tablespoons whole anise seed or about 2 teaspoons
    per cookie sheet (for sprinkling)
Additional cake flour (for dusting)

1. Stir 4 ½ cups cake flour, the baking powder, and salt together in a
   large bowl. Set aside for use in Step 5.

2. Place the eggs in the bowl of an electric mixer fitted with a paddle
   attachment and beat on medium speed until frothy and light, about
   5 minutes.

3. Turn the mixer to low speed and gradually add the powdered sugar,
   followed by the superfine sugar. Quickly scrape down the sides
   of the bowl and then resume beating at medium-high speed. Beat
   until the mixture is very thick and fluffy, about 10 minutes.

4. Turn the mixer to low speed. Add the lemon zest and anise extract,
   and mix well. Gradually add the melted butter and beat another 1 to
   2 minutes. (The mixture will lose some volume after the addition of
   the butter, but it should still be quite frothy and thick.)

5. Gradually add the flour mixture, blending just until combined. The
   dough will be sticky.

6. Turn the dough onto a well-floured work surface. Gently knead
   in enough flour to make a soft, smooth dough that doesn't stick to
   your hands. (The amount of additional flour will vary with egg size
   and humidity, but I generally use ½ to ¾ cup.)

7. Divide the dough into two equal portions and flatten each portion
   into a disk. Wrap each disk tightly in plastic and refrigerate about 1
   hour before rolling.

8. Line four cookie sheets with parchment paper and sprinkle them
   evenly with anise seed, using about 2 teaspoons per sheet.

9. Work with one half of the dough at a time, leaving the other half in
   the fridge until you are ready to use it. Using a regular rolling pin,
   roll the dough to a ¼- to ⅜-inch thickness on a well-floured work
   surface. *Note:* If your springerle mold or rolling pin is deeply cut,
   you may need to roll the dough thicker to capture the full imprint.

10. *If using a springerle mold to emboss:* Using a dry pastry brush,
    generously dust the mold with cake flour and press it facedown into
    the dough. Carefully lift up the mold. Cut around the imprint with
    a cookie cutter that nicely frames the imprint. Continue to press
    and cut, one cookie at a time, until all of the dough is used. *Note:* If
    you emboss a second cookie before cutting out the first, the act of
    embossing this cookie can distort the imprint on the first. **If using a
    springerle rolling pin to emboss:** Simply roll the dough again, now
    with the springerle rolling pin, and cut around the various cookies
    with a knife or pastry wheel.

    Repeat Steps 9 and 10 with the remaining dough. *Note:* If the
    dough sticks in the springerle mold or rolling pin, your dough may
    be too soft, you may not have adequately dusted the mold (or pin),
    or you may have pressed too hard. Brush out the mold (or pin) and
    start Step 9 again, using more flour to dust the top of the dough
    and the mold (or pin.) I try to use as little extra flour as possible
    since it can toughen dough. But to get a sharp imprint, springerle
    dough often needs more dusting than other rolled cookie dough.
    Also: Do not dust off excess flour on the cookie tops until the cook-
    ies have dried; otherwise, you may smudge the imprints.

11. Transfer the cookies to the prepared cookie sheets with an offset
    spatula, spacing them about 1 inch apart.

12. For the most distinct imprints, air-dry the cookies, uncovered, at
    least 8 to 10 hours before baking.

13. Position a rack in the center of the oven and preheat the oven to
    325 degrees F.

14. Bake 11 to 13 minutes (for 2 ¼-inch cookies), or until puffy, firm to
    the touch, and lightly browned on the bottom. The cookies should
    show minimal to no discoloration on top. Immediately transfer to
    wire racks and cool completely before storing. *Note:* Baking time
    varies considerably with cookie size and thickness.

Rosewater Marguerites
Makes about 4 dozen (1½-inch) cookies

These classy sandwiches of pistachio cookie, berry preserves, and soft meringue hark back to the turn of the century when ladies made a habit of indulging in high tea. A touch of rosewater makes them all the more fitting with this swap's garden theme.

Complexity:

Active Time:

Type: Rolled; piped; sandwich

Prep Talk: Allow 1 to 2 hours for the cookie dough to chill before rolling. The dough can be frozen up to 1 month with minimal loss of flavor if tightly wrapped in plastic and then foil. Store baked cookie bases at room temperature in airtight containers up to 1 week. However, once filled with preserves and topped with meringue, the cookies are best eaten within a few days. Because meringue quickly attracts moisture and gets sticky, package the finished marguerites in airtight containers as soon as they've cooled.

Pistachio Cookie Dough
1½ cups all-purpose flour, divided
¼ cup shelled pistachios (preferably salted), skins rubbed off
¼ teaspoon salt
2 large egg yolks, beaten
1½ tablespoons warm water
½ cup granulated sugar
½ cup (1 stick) unsalted butter, softened

¼ teaspoon pure rosewater (p. 156)

About 5 tablespoons seedless red raspberry jam (for filling)

Meringue Topping
3 large egg whites, room temperature
½ teaspoon strained freshly squeezed lemon juice
Pinch salt
2½ cups sifted powdered sugar
¾ teaspoon pure rosewater, or to taste
1 to 2 drops soft gel food coloring of your choice (optional, p. 152)

1. **Mix the Pistachio Cookie Dough.** Combine ½ cup flour and the pistachios in the bowl of a food processor fitted with a metal blade. Process until the nuts are finely ground but not pasty. Add the remaining flour and salt, and process until well combined. Set aside.

    Measure out 1½ tablespoons beaten egg yolk and combine with the water in the bowl of an electric mixer fitted with a whip attachment. (Discard the remaining yolk, or save for another use.) Beat 2 to 3 minutes on high speed, or until fluffy and lemon colored. Gradually add the sugar while still beating. Add the butter, a few tablespoons at a time, and beat until well blended. Scrape down the sides of the bowl as needed to ensure even mixing.

    Turn the mixer to low speed and add the rosewater. Gradually add the flour mixture, blending just until evenly incorporated.

2. Divide the dough into two equal portions and flatten each portion into a disk. Wrap each disk tightly in plastic and refrigerate 1 to 2 hours, or until firm enough to roll without sticking.

3. Position a rack in the center of the oven and preheat the oven to 375 degrees F. Line two cookie sheets with parchment paper.

4. Work with one disk of dough at a time. On a lightly floured surface, roll the dough to a ¼-inch thickness. Cut out small disks using a 1½-inch round cookie cutter and transfer the disks to the prepared cookie sheets, spacing them about 1 inch apart. Re-roll any dough scraps. Repeat with the remaining dough.

5. Bake the cookies 11 to 13 minutes, or until lightly browned around the edges. Immediately transfer to wire racks and cool completely before filling and topping.

6. **Top the cookies with jam.** Place a rounded ¼ teaspoon jam on the top center of each cookie. Spread the jam into a ¾- to 1-inch circle, taking care to keep it off the cookie edges.

7. Turn the oven down to 325 degrees F and re-line the two cookie sheets with parchment paper.

8. **Make the Meringue Topping.** Place the egg whites, lemon juice, and salt in the clean bowl of an electric mixer fitted with a whip attachment. (*Note:* The bowl, whip attachment, and all mixing utensils should be completely free of fat, or the egg whites will not reach full volume.) Beat on medium speed to soft peaks. Gradually add the powdered sugar, stopping to scrape down the sides of the bowl as often as needed. Turn the mixer to medium-high speed and continue to beat until the mixture is glossy and thick, about 7 to 10 more minutes. The meringue will not hold stiff peaks, but it should hold the "tracks" made by the beater. Add the rosewater in the last few minutes of beating, and the food coloring, if desired. *Note:* 1 to 2 drops of food coloring will make a very pale shade. Add more coloring for a deeper hue.

9. **Top the cookies.** Work quickly before the meringue deflates. Fit a pastry bag with a small (¼-inch) round tip and fill the bag with meringue. Pipe the meringue in concentric circles on top of each cookie. The meringue should completely cover the jam and come all the way to the cookie edge. If desired, smooth the meringue into a soft swirl by running your fingertip over the top in a circular motion. Quickly lift up your finger when it reaches the center to create a peak. Place the finished cookies about 1 inch apart on the prepared cookie sheets.

10. Bake the marguerites 6 to 7 minutes, or until the meringue is firm and dry but minimally discolored. Do not overbake, or the meringue may crack and separate from the cookie. Transfer the marguerites to wire racks and cool completely before serving or storing.

    Note: For an added treat, pipe any leftover meringue into small disks and bake as directed above.

A VISION IN WHITE

The months of May and June rarely come and go without at least one invitation to a bridal shower. While even newcomers to the wedding circuit know the basic shower routine quite well, there's no reason to let a proven party formula lull you into complacency. If ever there's a time to pull out all the stops, a once-in-a-lifetime wedding celebration is it. And this inventive cookie theme—a marriage of high style and sophisticated sweets—is just the way to give ho-hum bridal protocol a delicious and much-needed lift.

With soft hues, gracious styling, and subtle nut and citrus flavors, the cookies couldn't be better suited to this classy affair. Likewise, only unique—and taste-full—party games surface here. Make a friendly contest of cookie decorating by asking each partygoer to frost a cookie cake-topper shaped like a bride and groom. After the guest of honor declares the "Bride's Choice," give her an added win: tell her she can cherish the topper as long as she likes. (The simple storage tips on page 67 will keep her topper pristine well after it graces the wedding cake.)

When the bride opens her presents, sweeten the day even more. Turn the tables and shower guests with gifts too. Bejeweled photo albums used to file the party's recipes make wonderful keepsakes, as do cardboard boxes transformed into wedding cakes. Your friends and family will marvel over the luscious trims on the boxes, but the best icing of all will be the cookies they discover inside.

Cause to Celebrate:
A bridal shower, an intimate wedding reception or engagement party, a special wedding anniversary (especially silver or gold), a romantic couples' party.

Clockwise from bottom, Tiers of Joy, Bridal Veil Lace Wafers, Under Her Thumb(print) Cookies, Sugar Between the Sheets, Enduring Love Cookies, and (center) My Better Half Biscotti. Tiers of Joy (bottom center) and monogrammed sugar cookies (bottom right) bring in the requisite "something blue."

Top: Every swap needs at least one showstopper, such as these sugar cookies stenciled with the bride and groom's monogram. See page 154 for stenciling techniques.

Bottom: Inexpensive 4 x 6-inch photo albums are turned into glamorous recipe files with small silk flowers, rhinestone buttons, and mismatched costume jewelry. Customize the insides for each guest by pairing personal photos with the party's recipes.

Sugar Cookie Cake-Toppers

To make: Glue a decorated sugar cookie back to back with a decorated cookie of the same shape using thick Royal Icing. (The added cookie lends stability.) Then glue the two cookies to a round or oval cookie base, propping them straight up with crumpled paper towels or another lightweight object. Let the icing dry at least 1 hour before removing the props.

Notes: While bride and groom cookies are the obvious choice for cake-toppers, stenciled cookies and ones shaped like flower baskets (pictured above) are lovely as well. For custom cookie cutter and stencil sources, see page 156.

Toppers will stay firm and presentation-ready for several months if stored in airtight containers under cool, dry conditions. However, if you intend to eat them, it's best to do so within a week.

Wedding Cake Boxes

To make large tabletop boxes for display (pictured p. 64): Start with a set of three papier-mâché boxes of graduated size, differing in diameter by at least 3 or 4 inches. (Box sets are available in most craft stores and online, p. 156.) Set aside the lids; they will not be used here. Affix gift wrap, scrapbooking paper, and/or wallpaper to the sides of the boxes with spray adhesive. Use a glue gun to attach vintage lace, ribbons, strands of faux pearls, and/or other baubles to the top and bottom edges of each box. Stack the boxes, open ends facing up, using two smaller (about 4-inch-diameter) boxes as risers to separate the "tiers." Secure the boxes to one another with a glue gun; then line the insides with napkins or doilies before filling with cookies.

To make smaller boxes for take-home gifts (pictured above and opposite): Decorate the box lids as well as the sides, and glue the bottom of each box directly onto the lid of the box beneath it. This way, there's no need for unsightly plastic wrap, because the cookies stay completely covered.

Stand-ins

For a high-impact cookie display with less work, consider...

- Vintage hatboxes, left uncovered
- Footed cake stands, stacked one atop the other
- Plates elevated on candlesticks or vases to form one-of-a-kind pedestals
- Graduated stacks of dinner plates, salad plates, and saucers (stack like plates together, several plates high; then line the edge of the top plate in each stack with cookies)

Graceful vellum strips weave their way into Wedding Cake Boxes (p. 69), pointing the way to Sugar Between the Sheets and other cookie types.

Sugar Between the Sheets

Makes 4 dozen (2½-inch) crescents

This mélange of sugar and nuts rolled in sheets of flaky pastry is sexy enough at room temperature, but it's especially satisfying when hot.

Complexity:	Active Time:	Type:
		Rolled; hand-shaped

Prep Talk: The dough must be refrigerated 2 to 3 hours before it can be easily rolled without sticking. Store baked cookies in airtight containers at room temperature for 2 to 3 days. Cookies may also be prepared through Step 6 and frozen up to 1 month. When ready to serve, thaw on a prepared cookie sheet for 25 to 30 minutes, brush with lightly beaten egg white, and bake as directed.

Sour Cream Dough
2 cups all-purpose flour
¼ teaspoon salt
1 cup (2 sticks) unsalted butter, chilled and cut into
    tablespoon-size pieces
¾ cup sour cream
1 large egg, separated
1 teaspoon pure vanilla extract

Cinnamon-Walnut Filling
¾ cup granulated sugar
¾ cup walnut halves, toasted and cooled
1 teaspoon ground cinnamon

1. **Mix the Sour Cream Dough.** Stir the flour and salt together in a large bowl. Cut in the cold butter with a fork or pastry blender until it resembles very small peas.

   Whisk the sour cream, egg yolk, and vanilla extract together in another bowl. Make a well in the center of the dry ingredients and gradually stir in the sour cream mixture, blending just until combined. (A few butter lumps are perfectly fine. Avoid overmixing, as it will toughen the dough.)

2. Divide the dough into three equal portions. Flatten each portion into a disk and wrap each disk tightly in plastic. Refrigerate 2 to 3 hours or until the dough is quite firm.

3. **Make the Cinnamon-Walnut Filling.** Meanwhile, place the sugar, walnuts, and cinnamon in the bowl of a food processor fitted with a metal blade. Process until the nuts are finely ground but not pasty. Set aside.

4. Position a rack in the center of the oven and preheat the oven to 375 degrees F. Line two or more cookie sheets with parchment paper.

5. Work with one disk of dough at a time. On a lightly floured surface, roll the dough into a 12-inch circle, about ¹⁄₁₆ inch thick. Using a 12-inch cake pan or bowl as your guide, trim the dough to a uniform circle. Carefully pick up the edges of the dough and brush any excess flour off the back with a pastry brush. Sprinkle the top of the dough with one-third of the filling, taking care to cover the entire surface as evenly as possible. Gently press the filling into the dough.

6. With a sharp knife or pastry wheel, cut the circle into sixteen wedges. (For a fancier effect, use a fluted pastry wheel.) Starting at the widest end, roll up each wedge to form a crescent. (After each crescent is rolled, brush any scattered sugar mixture off the work surface so that it doesn't get on the outside of the next cookie.) Place the crescents, loose ends facing down, 1 to 2 inches apart on one of the prepared cookie sheets. Repeat Steps 5 and 6 with the remaining disks.

7. Whisk the egg white until slightly frothy and brush it evenly on top of each cookie. (If you plan to freeze the crescents, do not apply any egg white until after the cookies are thawed.)

8. Bake 15 to 17 minutes, or until lightly browned on the top and bottom. Eat warm from the oven for best flavor or transfer immediately to wire racks to cool.

My Better Half Biscotti

Makes 2 to 2 ½ dozen (1 x 4 ½-inch) biscotti

Every partnership benefits from the right balance of sugar and spice. Here the gentle heat of ginger is tempered with a creamy coating of sweet white chocolate. Together, they were meant to be.

Complexity:	Active Time:	Type:
		Hand-shaped

Prep Talk: Store in airtight containers in a cool, dry area up to 1 week. *Note:* The dipping chocolate will look its best if applied just before serving. It can turn dull and streaky if stored at temperatures in excess of 65 to 70 degrees F or under humid conditions. However, avoid refrigeration (except to set the chocolate); it will soften the cookies and dull the dragées.

1 recipe Basic Biscotti (p. 142)
⅓ cup lightly packed, finely minced crystallized ginger
2 teaspoons ground ginger
½ cup slivered almonds, lightly toasted, cooled, and finely chopped

1 pound premium white chocolate, melted (for dipping)

Decoration (optional)
About 2 tablespoons small (1 mm) silver dragées or 2 to 2 ½ dozen (3 mm) dragées (1 per cookie; p. 156)

1. Prepare 1 recipe Basic Biscotti as instructed on page 142, except add the crystallized and ground ginger to the flour mixture in Step 2. Break apart any pieces of crystallized ginger that may be stuck to one another. Add the almonds at the end of Step 4, shape the dough into loaves, and bake as directed. (Remember, do not overbake the loaves or let them cool for more than a few minutes, or they will be difficult to cut without cracking.)

2. Dip in chocolate. Line two cookie sheets with parchment paper and set aside. Pour the melted white chocolate into a 2-cup measuring cup to at least a 2½-inch depth. Dip one end of each biscotti into the white chocolate. Gently shake off any excess chocolate and then wipe the cookie bottom clean by dragging it along the edge of the measuring cup. (This will prevent a "foot" of chocolate from pooling around the biscotti.) Set the biscotti on a prepared cookie sheet and repeat with the remaining cookies. Do not let the cookies sit at room temperature for an extended period, or the chocolate can get dull and streaky. As soon as one sheet is full, proceed to Step 3, if desired, and then refrigerate as described in Step 4, below.

3. Decorate (optional). Work quickly before the chocolate sets. Fill a parchment paper cone with 1 mm dragées and cut a hole in the tip just large enough to allow the dragées to exit. Carefully deposit the beads in a thin line along the edge of the chocolate in the middle of each biscotti. (Alternatively, place one 3 mm dragée on each cookie.)

4. Refrigerate 10 to 15 minutes to allow the chocolate to set. Remove from the fridge and serve immediately, if possible, or store as directed.

    Note: There will be some leftover chocolate. Remove any crumbs by straining the chocolate through a sieve; then cover tightly and store at room temperature for another use.

Enduring Love Cookies

Makes about 5 dozen (1¾-inch) cookies

Almonds have been a longstanding symbol of love at weddings. Nearly 100 percent almond paste, this treat is closer to candy than cookie. It's no wonder kids fall head-over-heels for it too.

Complexity:	Active Time:	Type:
		Drop; hand-shaped

Prep Talk: Though the cookies may be made up to 1 week ahead, they will be their crunchiest if eaten within 24 hours. Store in airtight

1 pound almond paste, room temperature

2 cups granulated sugar

4 large egg whites

¼ teaspoon pure almond extract

3¼ cups slivered almonds, lightly toasted and cooled

Powdered sugar (as needed for dusting)

1. Place a rack in the center of the oven and preheat the oven to
   350 degrees F. Line two or more cookie sheets with parchment
   paper.

2. Using a food processor fitted with a metal blade, process the
   almond paste and sugar to a very fine crumb, about 1 minute. To
   encourage uniform processing, stop as needed to scrape down
   the sides of the bowl and to break apart any large masses of
   almond paste.

3. Place the egg whites in the bowl of an electric mixer fitted with
   a whip attachment and beat on medium-high speed until stiff
   but not dry. Add one-third of the whites to the almond paste
   mixture in the food processor and process until the mixture holds
   together in a smooth, soft mass. Stop and stir as needed to ensure
   uniform blending.

4. Turn the almond paste mixture into a large bowl and gently stir in
   the remaining whites along with the almond extract. Mix until uniformly blended. (The dough will be quite soft and sticky.)

5. Pour the slivered almonds into a large bowl or cake pan to form a
   shallow layer and set aside for use in Step 6.

6. For easiest shaping, work with a few cookies at a time. Portion the
   dough into small mounds using a rounded 1- to 1⅛-inch (#100)
   scoop or 1 rounded teaspoon per mound, and drop the mounds

directly into the slivered almonds. Sprinkle the cookie tops with
slivered almonds and roll to evenly coat. (The cookies will be less
likely to stick to your fingers if you first top them with nuts.)

7. Roll the balls between your palms to make perfect balls and to
   firmly fix the nuts in place. To prevent sticking, lightly dust your
   hands with powdered sugar as needed.

8. Place the balls 1 to 2 inches apart on the prepared cookie sheets
   and bake until lightly browned around the edges, about 15 to 18
   minutes. Cool a few minutes on the cookie sheets before transferring to wire racks; then cool completely before storing.

Bridal Veil Lace Wafers

Makes about 2 dozen (3½- to 3¾-inch)
wafers (or cylinders)

These thin cookies have the look of fine French lace. Let them cool
flat or roll them while still warm into statuesque arcs and cylinders. *Note:* These cookies are easiest to transport if they are left
unshaped. If you decide to shape them into cylinders or arcs, cradle
them in crumpled paper towels or pack them flush against one
another to keep them from rolling during transport. For long-term
storage, replace the paper towels with parchment paper so the
cookies stay their crispest. (Any moisture absorbed by the towels
will soften the cookies.)

Complexity:	Active Time:	Type:
❷	🕐	Drop; hand-shaped

Prep Talk: Silicone baking mats are recommended for this recipe,
though nonstick cookie sheets can be substituted (see Step 1, next
page). Store the wafers in airtight containers at room temperature
for 2 to 3 days. Contain them as soon as they've cooled. Due to their
high sugar content, they will quickly attract moisture and get soft if
not properly stored.

¼ cup all-purpose flour

¼ cup sliced almonds

⅝ teaspoon ground cardamom

⅛ teaspoon salt

¼ cup (½ stick) unsalted butter, softened

¼ cup granulated sugar

1 tablespoon heavy cream

1 tablespoon light corn syrup

1 tablespoon finely grated lemon zest

¾ teaspoon pure lemon oil (p. 156)

1. Position a rack in the center of the oven and preheat the oven to 350 degrees F. Line two or more cookie sheets with silicone baking mats. Alternatively, use nonstick cookie sheets. The cookies will look lacier and bake more quickly on nonstick cookie sheets, especially dark ones. However, a dark pan can make it more difficult to determine when the cookies are properly browned. (*Note:* With nonstick cookie sheets, no pan preparation is necessary. The cookies tend to misshape on parchment paper and will get doughy if baked on greased and floured pans.)

2. Place the flour, almonds, cardamom, and salt in the bowl of a food processor fitted with a metal blade. Process until the nuts are finely ground but not pasty.

3. Combine the butter, sugar, cream, and corn syrup in a medium (3-quart) nonreactive (stainless steel or coated) saucepan. Blend into a thick paste and set over medium-high heat, stirring as needed until the butter is melted. Bring the mixture to a rolling boil and let boil another 20 to 30 seconds.

4. Remove from the heat and stir in the lemon zest, oil, and flour mixture. Stir gently just until blended. (If you overstir, the butter may separate from the batter, but this is generally not a problem. Proceed as directed.)

5. Turn the batter into a bowl and let it cool until you can comfortably handle it, about 20 to 30 minutes. (The mixture will be quite loose at first but will thicken as it cools.) Drop the batter by rounded ½ teaspoonfuls onto the prepared (or nonstick) cookie sheets, placing no more than 5 cookies on each pan. (The cookies will spread to nearly three times their original diameter as they bake.) Reform any misshapen drops into rounds before they go in the oven. Again, if any butter separates from the dough at any point, don't worry. This will not cause problems.

6. Bake 7 to 9 minutes until golden brown, or closer to 5 to 7 minutes if you are using dark nonstick cookie sheets. Watch carefully, as the cookies go from golden to burned in a flash. Let the cookies cool 1 to 2 minutes on the cookie sheet, or until they can be picked up easily without falling apart.

7. Shape into arcs or cylinders (optional). Work with one cookie at a time, leaving the others on the cookie sheet so they stay warm and pliable. Drape the cookie over a rolling pin to form an arc. Or wrap it around a wooden dowel (about ⅞-inch diameter) to form a closed cylinder. Repeat with the remaining cookies. When the cookies have cooled enough to hold their shape, slide them off the end of the rolling pin or dowel. If the cookies should get brittle before you can shape them, return them to the oven for a few seconds and then try shaping them again.

8. Transfer to wire racks and cool completely before storing. (The cookies will at first appear oily, but as they cool, most of the buttery residue will disappear.) Wipe the silicone mats (or nonstick cookie sheets) clean of any excess butter before baking the next batch.

Under Her Thumb(print) Cookies

Makes 3½ to 4 dozen (1¾-inch) cookies

Monday night football and weekend golf with the guys are ordinarily stiff competition, but have no fear. Serve up this hazelnut thumbprint with a "kiss" of white chocolate on top, and you'll captivate him for good.

Complexity:

2

Active Time:

Type:

Drop; hand-shaped

Prep Talk: Unfilled cookies are best stored in airtight containers at room temperature up to 1 week. If filled, cookies should be stored in the fridge (the filling is perishable) and enjoyed within 2 to 3 days, before the cookies get soft.

Hazelnut Thumbprint Cookies

2 cups all-purpose flour

¼ cup lightly toasted chopped hazelnuts (with skins), cooled

½ teaspoon salt

1 cup (2 sticks) unsalted butter, slightly softened
½ cup firmly packed light brown sugar
2 large eggs, separated
2½ teaspoons pure hazelnut extract (p. 156)
1 teaspoon pure vanilla extract

1¾ cups untoasted chopped hazelnuts (with skins; for rolling)

White Chocolate–Hazelnut Ganache Filling
1 recipe Ganache, White Chocolate Variation (p. 150)
¾ teaspoon pure hazelnut extract

Decoration (optional)
About ¼ cup lightly toasted, coarsely chopped hazelnuts (with skins),
    cooled, or 3½ to 4 dozen large (3 mm) silver dragées (p. 156)

1. Position a rack in the center of the oven and preheat the oven to
   350 degrees F. Line two or more cookie sheets with parchment
   paper.

2. Mix the Hazelnut Thumbprint Cookies. Place the flour, hazelnuts,
   and salt in a food processor fitted with a metal blade. Process until
   the nuts are finely ground but not pasty.
       Place the butter and brown sugar in the bowl of an electric
   mixer fitted with a paddle attachment. Beat on medium speed
   until light and fluffy, about 1 to 2 minutes. Add the egg yolks and
   extracts. Continue to beat, scraping down the bowl as needed, until
   the mixture is well blended. Turn the mixer to low speed and gradually add the flour mixture, blending just until incorporated.

3. Finely chop the untoasted hazelnuts and place in a large bowl or
   cake pan to form a shallow layer.

4. Roll the dough between your palms into 1-inch balls. For the most
   uniform balls, first portion the dough into 1-inch mounds using a
   level 1⅜-inch (#70) scoop or 2 level teaspoons per mound; then
   roll into perfect balls. If the butter was overly soft to start, the dough
   may be sticky and hard to handle. Chill as needed until easily

shaped. Take care not to overchill, however, or the dough may
crack when you make the indentations in Step 6.

5. Place the egg whites in a small bowl and whisk until frothy. Work
   with one ball at a time. Lightly coat the ball with beaten egg white
   and then tumble in the untoasted hazelnuts to evenly coat. Roll
   between your palms again to firmly fix the nuts in place. Repeat
   with the remaining balls.

6. Arrange the cookies 1 to 2 inches apart on the prepared cookie
   sheets. Using your thumb or the end of a round-handled spoon,
   make a cup-shaped indentation in the center of each cookie.
   Bake 12 to 14 minutes, re-pressing the indentations midway
   through the baking process. When done, the cookies should be
   lightly browned on the bottom. Immediately transfer to wire racks
   to cool completely.

7. Prepare the White Chocolate–Hazelnut Ganache Filling. This
   filling will set if made too far in advance, so make it no sooner than
   you intend to fill the cookies. Follow the directions for Ganache,
   White Chocolate Variation (p. 150), stirring in the hazelnut
   extract at the very end. Cover with plastic wrap and chill about
   20 minutes, or until slightly thickened. Transfer to the bowl of
   an electric mixer fitted with a whip attachment. Beat on medium
   speed just until the ganache turns a shade whiter and holds the
   "tracks" left by the beater. Do not overbeat, or the ganache will
   break and become grainy.

8. Assemble the thumbprints. Work quickly before the ganache sets.
   Fit a pastry bag with a medium (⅜-inch) 6- to 8-pronged star tip
   and then fill the bag with the ganache. Hold the tip perpendicular
   to the cookie and pipe a rosette into the indentation by moving the
   bag in a tight circle. Quickly pull the bag up or to the side to form
   a delicate peak. (Alternatively, use a teaspoon to dollop the filling
   in the indentation.) Repeat with the remaining cookies. Top each
   cookie with a piece of coarsely chopped hazelnut or a single silver
   dragée if you prefer more glitz. Serve at room temperature.

Tiers of Joy

Makes about 1½ dozen (1½ to 1¾ x 1½-inch-tall) "cakes"

These diminutive wedding cakes are simply shortbread rounds frosted with Royal Icing and stacked large to small. To save time, omit the beaded borders or leave the cookies completely undecorated except for small sugar roses on top.

Complexity:	Active Time:	Type:
		Rolled

Prep Talk: The dough must be chilled 1 to 2 hours before rolling and cutting. The dough can be frozen up to 1 month with minimal loss of flavor if wrapped tightly in plastic and then foil. Store baked cookies in airtight containers at room temperature no longer than 2 weeks.

Orange Shortbread

1 recipe Shortbread, Straight Up (p. 143), sugar for sprinkling omitted
2 tablespoons finely grated orange zest
1 tablespoon pure orange extract

Orange Royal Icing

½ recipe Royal Icing (p. 151), thinned for top-coating (p. 152)
¾ teaspoon pure orange extract, or to taste
1 drop blue soft gel food coloring, or to desired shade (optional, p. 152)

Decoration (optional)

Water (as needed to thin icing)
Powdered sugar (as needed to thicken icing)
About 1½ dozen tiny (½-inch) ready-made royal icing roses
(1 per cake, p. 156)

1. Mix the Orange Shortbread. Prepare 1 recipe Shortbread, Straight Up, adding the orange zest and extract along with the vanilla extract in Step 2 (p. 143). Chill the dough and preheat the oven as directed.

2. On a lightly floured surface, roll the dough to a ³⁄₈-inch thickness. Cut out equal numbers of 1½-inch-, 1⅛-inch-, and ⁷⁄₈-inch- diameter rounds, arranging the largest ones on one parchment paper–lined cookie sheet and the two smaller ones on another. Do not sprinkle with sugar as instructed in Shortbread, Straight Up, as the sugar will make it more difficult to top-coat the cookies in Step 4, below. Bake the largest rounds 25 to 28 minutes and the two smaller rounds 20 to 23 minutes. Cool as directed on p. 143.

3. Prepare the Orange Royal Icing. Prepare ½ recipe Royal Icing, thinned for top-coating (p. 152), mixing in the orange extract at the end. Reserve about ¾ cup icing for the cake borders. (Remember to cover the surface of the icing flush with plastic wrap when not in use; otherwise, a crust will quickly form.) To the remainder of the icing, add a drop of blue food coloring, if desired, to make a pale shade. Mix well.

4. Top-coat the cookies. Work with one cookie at a time. Using the handle-end of a clean craft paintbrush (about ¼-inch diameter), apply a small amount of icing to the top center of the cookie. Working quickly before the icing sets, spread the icing across the cookie top with the tip of the handle. Once the cookie is smoothly coated, set it aside to dry at least 3 hours. Repeat with the remaining cookies.

5. Assemble the cakes. Create tiered cakes by stacking the cookies three high, starting with the 1½-inch disk on the bottom and ending with the ⁷⁄₈-inch disk on the top. Secure each cookie to the next with a dab of leftover icing. Allow the icing to set 20 to 30 minutes before adding the borders.

6. Decorate (optional). Fill a parchment paper cone with the reserved white icing and cut a small (⅛-inch) hole in the tip. Hold the bag perpendicular to the cookie and apply gentle pressure. A smooth, well-rounded dot should form without much spreading. If the dot forms a peak when you pull up on the bag, empty the bag into a small bowl and slowly add water to loosen the icing. (Conversely, if the dot spreads, thicken the icing by gradually adding powdered sugar.) Pipe a series of tiny dots around the edge of each cookie and let dry. If desired, glue a small ready-made royal icing rose on top of each cookie with leftover icing.

    Note: There will be leftover Royal Icing. Cover and store as directed (p. 151) for another use.

BEACH

CAMP

Lemon-Lime
Sugar Cookies

Top Dogs

FUN IN THE SUN

It's steaming hot, and the long, lazy days of summer are settling into a slow and steady rhythm that calls for chilling out with family and friends. Supplement your next backyard barbeque or picnic at the shore with this whimsical swap, splashed with playful colors and sunny citrus flavors.

From the sunglasses and bathing suits strewn on the edible beach to the hot dogs and burgers at rest on the grill, this party's treats deliver a generous helping of summertime cheer. For more fun and games, you needn't look beyond the cookies. In advance of the party, hide mismatched pairs of flip-flop cookies in the yard; then give each guest the other half of several sets. The challenge: the first to find all the right partners gets to fill her beach tote with cookies before the rest. Alternatively, bury well-wrapped cookies in piles of bread or cookie crumbs, hand kids plastic shovels, and let the search for sunken treasures begin. For children who are more artistic than adventurous, fill plastic squeeze bottles with red and yellow Italian Buttercream and watch the creative fireworks as they add their own fixin's to Top Dogs and Chocolate-Chai Burgers.

Whether your summer entertaining philosophy tends toward low-key or all-out, you're in luck. This party is infinitely adaptable too. To scale back, skip the games. Not simple enough? Then let go of the painted sand-pail displays or the customized beach totes for carrying leftovers home. After all, this is one swap where paper plates and plastic cups fit right in.

Cause to Celebrate:
Memorial Day, summer solstice, Fourth of July, a family reunion, a July or August birthday (especially for a young child), Labor Day.

Clockwise from top left, Lemon-Lime Sugar Cookies, S'mores Brownies, Lemonade Slices, Chocolate-Chai Burgers, and Top Dogs. Not pictured: Chocolate Chip Watermelon Wedges and Piña Colada Beach Balls.

Top left: Lemon-Lime Sugar Cookie swimsuits are painted in lively hues and dotted with fondant appliqué. See page 149 for the lemon-lime variation of Signature Sugar Cookie Dough and page 154 for appliqué techniques.

Opposite: Plumped with terrycloth remnants and Lemon-Lime Sugar Cookies, tiny straw totes settle into a cookie crumb sand dune. Castaway buttons, salvaged shells, and ribbons embroidered with guests' names add personality to these take-home gifts.

Fan-tastic Invitations *(bottom left)*

To make: Photocopy a summertime image onto a piece of cardstock. Write or print the party's place, date, and time on top. Cut the image into a fan shape. Print a favorite cookie recipe on another piece of cardstock and cut it out to match the first fan shape. Using a glue gun, mount the top 1 to 2 inches of a large (1 x 8-inch-long) flat wood craft stick (available at most craft stores) to the back of one of the fan shapes. Affix the remaining fan shape to the back of the first one with spray adhesive, taking care to line up the two shapes. Let the fan dry several hours, weighted flat between books. Attach embellishments, such as shells and ribbons, with a glue gun. Package fans in padded envelopes before mailing.

Beachy Keen

To make "sand" for a tabletop "dune" (opposite and top left) or to fill a sand-pail display (bottom left; also p. 80): Grind store-bought graham crackers into a fine crumb in a food processor. Add color and texture variation to the sand by sprinkling regular granulated or coarse-grained white sugar on top. *Note:* You'll need surprisingly few crackers—less than one box fills two or more 8-inch pails if you first fit the pails with false Styrofoam bottoms.

me
Cookies

Piña Colada
Beach Balls

To help guests identify their picnic pleasure, arrange like cookies in buckets spray-painted in bold nautical stripes; then embroider cookie names on beach towels or ribbons, and tuck them next to the appropriate treat.

Piña Colada Beach Balls

Makes 1½ to 2 dozen (2¾- to 3-inch) cookies

The fresh flavors of everyone's favorite summer cocktail are mixed up in Classic Icebox Cookie Dough to create what's sure to be the life of the party. The dough can be shaped into beach balls, as I've done here, or into a host of other clever forms. For a patriotic "stars and stripes" twist, perfect for Independence Day, fashion it into pinstripes (p. 145), slice, and then cut into stars or squares.

Complexity: Active Time: Type: Hand-shaped; icebox

Prep Talk: For best results, the dough must be chilled for 1 to 2 hours before shaping and then for another 1 to 2 hours before slicing—so plan accordingly. Shaped dough can be stored in the freezer up to 1 month with minimal loss of flavor if tightly wrapped in plastic and then foil. When you're ready for cookies, simply slice and bake. Store baked cookies in airtight containers up to 5 days. For the crunchiest eating, enjoy within 24 hours.

1 recipe Classic Icebox Cookie Dough (p. 144)

1½ teaspoons coconut extract

1 cup lightly packed sweetened coconut flakes (optional)

½ cup dried pineapple pieces, about 1 (3-ounce) bag (optional)

20 to 25 drops soft gel food coloring of your choice, or to desired shade (p. 152)

1. Prepare 1 recipe Classic Icebox Cookie Dough through Step 3 (p. 144), adding the coconut extract along with the vanilla extract. Process the coconut flakes and pineapple pieces to a fine meal in a food processor fitted with a metal blade, and stir into the finished dough, if desired.

2. Reserve 1 tablespoon dough for use in Step 4, right. Divide the remaining dough in half. To the first half, add the food coloring and mix well to evenly distribute the color. Leave the second half as-is.

3. Follow the instructions in Steps 5 and 6 (p. 144) for chilling, shaping, and freezing the dough for Beach Balls. *Note:* If you add the coconut flakes and pineapple, the logs will be closer to 5 inches rather than 4 inches long.

4. Slice and bake the dough as directed in Steps 7 to 10 (p. 144), except before baking the cookies, shape the reserved tablespoon of dough into tiny (¼-inch) balls and gently press one into the center of each cookie to make a "button." (*Note:* If a log should pop apart when slicing it into cookies, split it in half lengthwise. Cut two half-circles from each half-log and piece them together on the cookie sheet into a complete circle. Repeat for the remaining cookies.) For perfectly round cookies, you can either trim with a 2¼-inch round cutter before baking or with a 2¾-inch round cutter after baking, while the cookies are still hot. If the cookies aren't sliced to a uniform thickness before baking, they can spread unevenly. When this occurs, I trim after baking.

Lemonade Slices

Makes 3½ to 4 dozen (1¾ x 3¼-inch) lemon slices

Tantalizingly tart, these sunny yellow citrus slices are sure to brighten your swap. *Note:* This cookie is high on lemon flavor. For kids, adjust the lemon flavorings to taste or make plain vanilla dough as instructed on page 144.

Complexity: Active Time: Type: Hand-shaped; rolled; icebox

Prep Talk: For best results, the dough must be chilled for 1 to 2 hours before shaping and then for another 1 to 2 hours before slicing—so plan accordingly. Shaped dough can be stored in the freezer up to 1 month with minimal loss of flavor if tightly wrapped in plastic and then foil. When you're ready for cookies, simply slice and bake. Store baked cookies in airtight containers up to 5 days. For the crunchiest eating, enjoy within 24 hours.

Lemonade Slices (left) and Chocolate Chip Watermelon Wedges (right)

1 recipe Classic Icebox Cookie Dough (p. 144) less
    ¼ teaspoon baking soda
1 tablespoon finely grated lemon zest
1½ tablespoons strained freshly squeezed lemon juice
2¼ teaspoons pure lemon oil (p. 156)
About 15 drops yellow soft gel food coloring, divided, or to
    desired shade (p. 152)

Decoration (optional)
½ recipe Royal Icing (p. 151), thinned for beadwork (p. 152)

1. Prepare 1 recipe Classic Icebox Cookie Dough through Step 3
    (p. 144), but reduce the baking soda by ¼ teaspoon and add the
    lemon zest, juice, and oil along with the vanilla extract.

2. Portion off two-thirds of the dough. Add 3 to 4 drops yellow food

coloring to tint it pale yellow and mix well to evenly distribute the
color.

3. Divide the remaining dough in half. To one half, add 10 to 12 drops
    yellow food coloring to tint it deep yellow. Again, mix well. Leave
    the remaining half un-tinted.

4. Flatten the three colors of dough into separate disks and wrap each
    disk tightly in plastic. Chill the light yellow dough 1 to 2 hours before
    shaping into a log in Step 5, below; chill the other two disks closer
    to 2 hours before rolling in Steps 6 and 7, next page.

5. On a lightly floured surface, shape the light yellow dough into a
    6½-inch-long log, about 2½ inches in diameter. Wrap the log
    tightly in plastic to hold its shape and set in the freezer until ready to
    use in Step 6. (Stand on end to prevent flattening on one side.)

6. Roll the white dough into a 6½ x 6- to 7-inch rectangle, about ³⁄₁₆ inch thick. Carefully wrap it around the light yellow log, trimming off any excess white dough where the ends meet and also at the ends of the log.

7. Roll the dark yellow dough into a 6½ x 8- to 9-inch rectangle, about ¹⁄₁₆ to ⅛ inch thick, and wrap it around the log as instructed above. (If needed, brush the dough lightly with egg wash [p. 144] so it sticks to the log.) Wrap the log tightly in plastic and freeze, standing on end, 1 to 2 hours or until quite firm.

8. Slice the log in half lengthwise. Lay one half-log flat side down on a cutting board and cut it crosswise into ³⁄₁₆- to ¼-inch-thick slices. (Keep the second half in the freezer while you work.) Transfer the slices to a parchment paper–lined cookie sheet. Repeat with the remaining half-log.

9. (Optional) While the dough is still quite firm, mark the "lemon sections" by cutting 2 to 3 small (⅛- to ³⁄₁₆-inch) wedges out of the pale yellow portion of each slice. (In the heat of the oven, the dough on both sides of each wedge will spread into the void and join together to form a thin line.) If the cookies have gotten too soft to easily cut, return to the refrigerator until they are firm.

10. Bake and cool as indicated on page 144. While the cookies are still warm, trim the "cut" edge of the lemon slice, if desired.

11. Decorate (optional). Fill a parchment paper cone with Royal Icing, thinned for beadwork (p. 152), and cut a small (⅛- to ¼-inch) hole in the tip. Pipe 2 to 3 small "seeds" on top of each lemon slice. Let the icing dry before serving.

Variation: Chocolate Chip Watermelon Wedges

Makes 3½ to 4 dozen (2½ x 4½-inch) wedges

Note: Again, this cookie is high on citrus flavor. For younger folks, adjust the lime flavorings to taste or make plain vanilla dough (p. 144).

1. Prepare 2 recipes Classic Icebox Cookie Dough through Step 3 (p. 144), adding 1 tablespoon pure lime oil and 2 teaspoons finely grated lime zest along with the vanilla extract. Divide the dough in half.

2. Combine the first half of dough with one-quarter of the second half. Add 3 to 5 drops red soft gel food coloring to the combined mass to tint it pink (or add more coloring for a darker red.)

3. Divide the remaining dough into two portions, one about twice the size of the other. To the smaller portion, add 7 to 10 drops green soft gel food coloring to tint it dark green. Leave the larger portion un-tinted.

4. Chill as directed for Lemonade Slices (Step 4, p. 86), about 1 to 2 hours for the red dough and closer to 2 hours for the green and plain dough.

5. On a lightly floured surface, shape the red dough into a 6½-inch-long log, about 3 inches in diameter. Wrap the log tightly in plastic to hold its shape and set in the freezer until ready to use in Step 6, below. (Stand on end to prevent flattening on one side.)

6. Roll the white dough into a 6½ x 10- to 11-inch rectangle, about ¼ to ⅜ inch thick, and wrap it around the outside of the red log. Trim any excess white dough where the ends meet and also at the ends of the log.

7. Roll the remaining green dough into a 6½ x 14- to 15-inch rectangle, about ¹⁄₁₆ inch thick, and wrap it around the log. Trim any excess green dough.

8. Freeze, cut, and bake as directed for Lemonade Slices, but before baking, add "watermelon seeds" by studding the red part of each wedge with 8 to 10 mini chocolate chips. Baking time will be closer to 10 minutes due to the generous size of the cookie.

S'mores Bars

Makes 2 dozen (2-inch) squares

I've taken the same campy ingredients in s'mores and turned them into an easy-to-package bar, perfect for tossing into summer picnic baskets.

Complexity: Active Time: Type:

          Bar

Prep Talk: Allow about 1 hour for the brownies to cool before applying the marshmallow topping; otherwise, the marshmallows will melt and flatten. The brownies will stay fresh longer if kept in the pan, tightly wrapped in foil, and cut just before serving. Store at room temperature up to 1 week.

Graham Cracker Crust

2 ¼ cups graham cracker crumbs (15 to 17 crackers, finely ground
   in a food processor)
¼ cup granulated sugar
2 tablespoons firmly packed light brown sugar
¾ cup (1½ sticks) unsalted butter, melted

Fudge Brownie Filling

6 ounces premium unsweetened chocolate, chopped
1 cup (2 sticks) plus 2 tablespoons unsalted butter, chopped into
   tablespoon-size pieces
2½ cups granulated sugar
5 large eggs, lightly beaten
1½ teaspoons pure vanilla extract
1¾ cups all-purpose flour

1½ cups pecan halves, toasted and coarsely chopped (optional,
   for topping)
4 cups (packed) miniature marshmallows (about 8 ounces,
   for topping)

1. Line a 10 x 15 x 2-inch glass baking dish (sometimes called a roasting pan, p. 10) with foil, leaving a 1-inch overhang around the top edge of the pan. Smooth out any big wrinkles in the foil and then lightly coat the foil with nonstick cooking spray.

2. Position a rack in the center of the oven and preheat the oven to 350 degrees F.

3. Prepare the Graham Cracker Crust. Combine the graham cracker crumbs and sugars in a small bowl. Gradually add the melted butter until the crumbs just hold together when squeezed in your palm. (The crumbs may absorb slightly more or less butter depending on the graham cracker brand.) Press the mixture into an even ¼-inch-thick layer on the bottom of the prepared pan. Run a smooth-bottomed measuring cup over the crust to pack and level it.

4. Mix the Fudge Brownie Filling. Combine the chocolate and butter in a large bowl (about 4-quart capacity) that fits a double boiler. Place the bowl over barely simmering water and stir as needed until the chocolate and butter are melted. Remove from the heat and whisk in the sugar, followed by the beaten eggs and vanilla extract. Stir in the flour, mixing until smooth. Pour the batter on top of the graham cracker crust and level with a small offset spatula.

5. Top and bake. Scatter the chopped nuts evenly over the batter, if desired. Bake 30 to 35 minutes, or until a cake tester inserted in the brownie center comes out with dark, damp crumbs on it. Do not overbake. Set on a wire rack and cool completely in the pan.

6. Distribute the marshmallows evenly over the brownie top. Place the pan under the broiler in the top third of the oven for about 1 minute, or until the marshmallows are puffy and golden brown. Watch carefully and rotate the pan regularly, as the marshmallows can easily burn. Cool until the topping is firm and easily cut without sticking.

7. Remove the brownies from the pan in one block by gently pulling up on the foil overhang or by easing the block out with an offset spatula. Place directly on a cutting board. Remove all foil and trim any uneven edges before cutting into 2-inch squares. For the neatest cuts, use a sharp knife, wiped clean with a warm, damp cloth between slices.

Set atop a small grill, Top Dogs (left) and Chocolate-Chai Burgers on Sesame Seed Buns (right) are completely in tune with this party's theme.

Chocolate-Chai Burgers on Sesame Seed Buns

Makes about 1½ dozen (1½- to 1¾-inch) "burgers"

The stately *macaron* (French for macaroon) has never been so fun! *Note:* Though short on ingredients, the macaron is long on technique. Pay close attention to the mixing and drying instructions to achieve the cookie's characteristic smooth dome and crinkly foot.

Complexity:	Active Time:	Type:
		Piped; sandwich

Prep Talk: Store unfilled macaron "buns" in airtight containers at room temperature up to 2 weeks. Once filled, the cookies must be refrigerated. (The filling is perishable.) Store in airtight containers in the fridge for 2 to 3 days. For best flavor and texture, bring to room temperature before serving.

Cocoa Macaron "Buns"

1¼ cups powdered sugar

1 cup almond flour (aka almond meal, available at organic
   and health food stores)

2 tablespoons unsweetened Dutch-process cocoa powder

3 large egg whites, room temperature

⅛ teaspoon salt

¼ cup sifted superfine sugar

1 to 1½ teaspoons white sesame seeds (for sprinkling)

Chai-Infused Ganache "Burgers"

1 recipe Ganache (p. 149), chocolate reduced to 9 ounces

10 Chai tea bags

1. Position a rack in the center of the oven and preheat the oven to 325 degrees F. Line two cookie sheets with parchment paper.

2. Mix the Cocoa Macaron "Buns." Using a large-gauge sieve, sift the powdered sugar, almond flour, and cocoa powder together in a medium bowl. Break apart any lumps of almond flour remaining in the sieve and add to the bowl.

   Place the egg whites in the clean bowl of an electric mixer fitted with a whip attachment. (*Note:* The bowl, whip attachment, and all mixing utensils should be completely free of fat, or the egg whites will not stiffen.) Beat on medium speed until frothy and then add the salt. Turn the mixer to high speed and continue to beat to firm peaks, less than 1 minute. With the mixer still running, gradually add the superfine sugar. Stop briefly, if needed, to scrape any sugar off the sides of the bowl; then continue beating until the whites are stiff and shiny, about 1 more minute. Do not overbeat, as you'll find it more difficult to incorporate the dry ingredients, below, without overfolding.

   Remove the bowl from the mixer and transfer the whites to a large bowl. Sift the almond flour mixture over the top of the meringue in three additions, folding with a large rubber spatula between each addition. Stop folding just as soon as the dry ingredients are evenly incorporated and the batter has turned shiny. The batter should be thick, but peaks created by lifting up the spatula should largely disappear into the bulk of the batter. (It is normal for the meringue to deflate quite a bit after the dry ingredients are added.)

3. Turn the meringue into a pastry bag fitted with a ⅜-inch round tip. Pipe the batter into 1½- to 1¾-inch rounds onto the prepared cookie sheets, spacing the cookies about 1 inch apart. Rap the cookie sheets on a tabletop to release trapped air bubbles. Flatten any peaks in the meringue with a barely damp fingertip and sprinkle the cookie tops evenly with sesame seeds.

4. Air-dry until a skin has formed on the cookie tops, about 30 to 45 minutes. (Drying time will vary with humidity and air temperature. When ready, the macarons will have lost some of their stickiness and sheen. I often accelerate the process by blowing the cookie tops with my hair dryer.)

5. Bake 13 to 15 minutes. When done, the cookies should feel dry and firm and should begin to lift off the parchment paper when gently nudged. (If the cookies do not budge from the paper, bake 1 to 2 minutes longer.) Slide the cookies, still on the parchment paper, onto a wire rack and cool a few minutes until they are easily removed from the paper. Cool completely before filling or storing.

6. Prepare the Chai-Infused Ganache "Burgers." It is best to make the ganache just before you're ready to assemble the cookies. (If made in advance, it must be refrigerated and then softened at room temperature to the proper working consistency.) Prepare 1 recipe Ganache as instructed on pages 149 and 150, but reduce the chocolate to 9 ounces. At the end of Step 2, add the tea bags to the warm cream and let them steep 30 minutes. Before proceeding to Step 3, rewarm the cream over medium heat.

    After straining the cream onto the chocolate, gently squeeze the tea bags through the sieve to release the retained cream. Discard the spent tea bags. Proceed as directed, chilling the ganache to piping consistency in Step 4.

7. Assemble the sandwiches. Transfer the chilled ganache to a pastry bag fitted with a 1/8-inch round tip. The ganache should be sufficiently thick to hold a thin line when piped. If not, empty the pastry bag and return the ganache to the fridge for additional chilling. (Note: If the ganache is too thick to easily pipe, warm it with your hands by squeezing the bag repeatedly.) Turn half of the cookies over so the bottoms are facing up. Pipe a 1¾-inch-diameter mound, about ¼ inch tall, on each cookie bottom. The more squiggles you pipe, the more closely the mound will resemble a hamburger patty. (As a time-saver, the ganache can also be spooned onto the cookies.) Cap with another cookie of similar size and gently press together to form a sandwich.

    Note: There will be some leftover ganache. Store in the fridge or freezer, as directed on page 150, for another use.

Top Dogs with Coffee Cream Filling

Makes 2 to 2 ½ dozen (2 ½-inch) sandwich cookies

Here's another backyard barbeque look-alike to take your summer swap over the top. To streamline the preparation of these dogs, mix and bake the meringue "buns" ahead; then fill them right before serving. *Note:* For a more kid-friendly filling, increase the vanilla extract in Italian Buttercream to 1 tablespoon and substitute 2 ounces melted, cooled semisweet chocolate for the espresso powder in Step 5, below.

Complexity:	Active Time:	Type:
2		Piped; sandwich

Prep Talk: Store unfilled meringue "buns" in airtight containers at room temperature up to 2 weeks. Once filled, the cookies must be refrigerated. (The filling is perishable.) Store in airtight containers in the fridge for 2 to 3 days. For best eating, serve at room temperature. *Note:* The buns will be quite crunchy to start. If you prefer a softer texture, allow the cookies to sit for 1 to 2 days in the fridge before serving.

Hazelnut Meringue "Buns"
1 cup granulated sugar, divided
¾ cup chopped hazelnuts (with skins)
2 tablespoons cornstarch
4 large egg whites, room temperature
¼ teaspoon cream of tartar
⅛ teaspoon salt
½ teaspoon pure hazelnut extract (p. 156)

Coffee Buttercream Filling
2 cups (about ½ recipe) Italian Buttercream (p. 150), divided
15 to 20 drops yellow soft gel food coloring (p. 152)
15 to 20 drops brown soft gel food coloring, divided
1½ tablespoons instant espresso powder, dissolved in 1 teaspoon boiling water
1 to 2 drops red soft gel food coloring

1. Position racks in the upper and lower thirds of the oven and preheat the oven to 300 degrees F. (If you have two ovens, position racks in the middle and preheat both ovens. The cookies will bake more evenly in this configuration.) Line two cookie sheets with parchment paper.

2. Mix the Hazelnut Meringue "Buns." Combine ½ cup sugar, the hazelnuts, and cornstarch in the bowl of a food processor fitted with a metal blade. Process until the nuts are finely ground but not pasty.

   Place the egg whites and cream of tartar in the clean bowl of an electric mixer fitted with a whip attachment. (*Note:* The bowl, whip attachment, and all mixing utensils should be completely free of fat, or the egg whites will not stiffen.) Beat on medium speed until frothy and add the salt. Continue to beat to firm peaks. Turn the mixer to medium-high speed and gradually add the remaining sugar. Quickly scrape down the sides of the bowl; then resume beating on high speed until the whites are stiff and glossy, about 1 to 2 minutes.

   Using a large rubber spatula, fold in the nut mixture along with the hazelnut extract.

3. Turn the meringue into a pastry bag fitted with a ½-inch round tip. Pipe 2 to 2½ dozen small (¾ x 2¼-inch) buns onto each of the prepared cookie sheets, spacing the cookies about 1 inch apart. (You should have 4 to 5 dozen buns in total, 2 per finished cookie.) Smooth any peaks in the meringue with a barely damp fingertip. *Note:* There will be leftover batter; but if it isn't baked immediately after piping, it will quickly lose volume.

4. Place both cookie sheets in the oven at the same time and bake 25 to 30 minutes, or until the cookies are crisp and lightly browned. To ensure even browning, rotate the cookie sheets from top to bottom rack, and vice versa, midway through baking. (Alternatively, place one cookie sheet in each of two ovens.) Immediately transfer the cookies to wire racks and cool completely before filling or storing.

5. Mix the Coffee Buttercream Filling. It is best to make the buttercream just before you're ready to assemble the cookies. (If made in advance, it must be refrigerated and then softened at room temperature to the proper working consistency.) Mix ½ cup Italian Buttercream with the yellow food coloring and a drop of brown coloring to make the "mustard." Combine the remaining 1½ cups Italian Buttercream with the dissolved espresso powder (or 2 ounces melted, cooled semisweet chocolate for kids) and whisk well. Deepen the color to a hot dog hue by adding the remaining brown and red food coloring.

6. Assemble the cookies. Fit a pastry bag with a ⅜-inch round tip and fill with the brown buttercream. Fit another pastry bag with a ⅛-inch round tip and fill with the yellow buttercream. Turn half of the cookies flat side up. Using the first pastry bag, pipe a short (½ x 1¾-inch) "hot dog" along the length of each cookie. Top each hot dog with another bun, placed flat side down, and gently press together. Turn the sandwiches on their sides so that the hot dogs are clearly visible from the top. Using the second pastry bag, pipe a squiggle of yellow buttercream on top of each hot dog to mimic a squirt of mustard.

COOKIES CUM LAUDE

Now that summer vacation is over and the kids are back in school, moms can finally enjoy some long-awaited downtime—in between carpools, PTA meetings, and helping with homework, that is. Make the most of your extra minutes with this back-to-school cookie swap. After all, there are few other events where you can relax with friends and simultaneously stock up on afternoon snacks for your kids.

This party's lesson in entertaining begins with an invitation crafted from a recycled report card—a touch that's sure to earn high marks in creativity. At the swap, the education continues. Vintage lunchboxes stand in for the usual plates; copies of class portraits serve as lunchbox liners; and a blackboard and scattered workbook pages form a patchwork "tablecloth." Fast, no-trouble cookies dominate the desktop display and fulfill the prerequisites for multi-tasking moms. Loaded with chocolate, peanut butter, caramel, and other ingredients that kids love, these goodies are just as likely to please the partygoers as the folks waiting at home.

To make this swap even smarter, hand out compact composition books or pencil pouches filled with blank index cards. As guests gather their cookies to go, they'll be happy to have paper nearby for jotting down recipes from their baker-friends.

Cause to Celebrate:
Back-to-school, an autumn birthday (especially for scholarly sorts), Labor Day, a class reunion, a graduation.

Clockwise from lower right, The Brown(ie)-Noser; Gold Star Macaroons; Teacher's Pet; No-Hassle, No-Bake Oatmeal Fudge Cookies; Brain Teaser; and (center) Peanut Butter and Jelly Sandwiches.

Report Card Invitations *(top right)*

To make: Choose an old report card (the less that's been written on it, the better). Digitally scan both the inside and outside and then modify the scanned card with photo-editing software to include the party's date, place, time, and other essential cookie swap tips, such as how many cookies to bring. Print out both sides of the card back to back, trim the invitation to size, and fold it in half. Enclose finished invitations in manila envelopes decorated with foil stars.

Note-worthy Recipe Books *(below)*

To make: Print or write guests' names on strips of cardstock and glue each strip to the front of a pocket-size composition book (available in office supply stores or online). Loop shorter strips around small pencils; then affix the strips to the inside back covers. If you've collected the recipes in advance, print them on notebook paper and glue them into the books as well. Just be sure to leave plenty of extra pages for note-taking.

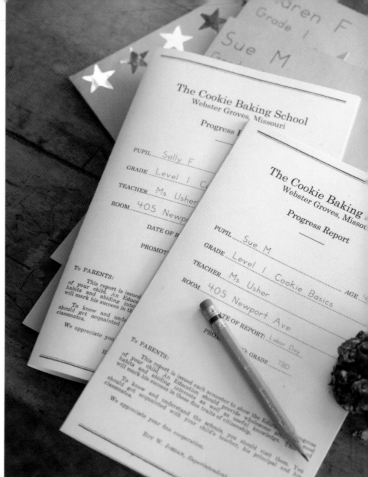

Left: To keep Royal Icing top coats contained on petite cookies, such as these letters, or to fill small angular spaces on larger cookies, the flooding technique (p. 153) is the way to go. Consistency is king when applying details to top coats. A relatively thick Royal Icing is preferred for piping sharp, well-defined lines, as on "LEE," whereas a thinner consistency is best for dots (aka beadwork, p. 153), like those on "SALLY." For consistency adjustments to Royal Icing, see pages 151–152.

Take-Home Book Boxes *(bottom left)*

To make these cookie containers: Cover a papier-mâché book box (available online, p. 156, and in craft stores) with scrapbooking papers and/or photocopies of old book covers. Use spray adhesive for large surfaces and decoupage glue for small curved areas along the spine. Avoid placing paper over the joint where the cover meets the spine. Print a table of contents that lists each cookie by name and glue to the inside front cover, or mount a self-adhesive envelope in the same place and fill with recipe cards. Let the boxes dry thoroughly before lining with parchment paper and filling with cookies. (The parchment paper will keep the oils in the cookies from staining the box.) For added oomph, personalize the boxes with guests' names spelled in Cinnamon Sugar Cookie (p. 149) letters, aptly flavored for the fall season.

Stand-ins

Other take-away containers with a scholarly bent, only quicker . . .

- Plain tin lunchboxes. Some thoughtfully applied paint or pretty paper will contribute the needed character.

- Brown paper lunch sacks embellished with a name tag or grade school portrait of each guest.

- Clear plastic pouches ordinarily used for pencils and other school supplies.

Teacher's Pet

Makes 2 ½ to 3 dozen (2 ½-inch) cookies

When a simple apple no longer satisfies, try these overstuffed apple-spice cookies on for size. *Note:* Feel free to alter the mix-ins to satisfy your kids.

Complexity:

1

Active Time:

Type:

Drop

Prep Talk: Store in airtight containers at room temperature for 3 to 4 days. Due to its fruit content, this cookie is soft and will only get softer after the first day. Eat freshly baked to enjoy a crunchy exterior.

2 cups all-purpose flour

2 ½ teaspoons ground cinnamon

½ teaspoon baking soda

½ teaspoon salt

¾ cup plus 3 tablespoons firmly packed light brown sugar

½ cup (1 stick) plus 2 tablespoons unsalted butter, softened

1 large egg

¼ cup apple cider (or juice), room temperature

1 ½ teaspoons pure vanilla extract

1 ¼ cups peeled, cored, and chopped apples (1 to 2 tart cooking
    apples, such as Granny Smith, cut into ¼-inch dice)

1 cup walnut halves, lightly toasted and chopped

1 cup pitted, chopped dates (stems removed, cut into ¼-inch dice)

½ cup butterscotch morsels

Apple Cider Glaze (optional)

3 cups powdered sugar, sifted

1 tablespoon strained freshly squeezed lemon juice

About 4 tablespoons apple cider (or juice)

Powdered sugar (as needed to thicken glaze)

1. Position a rack in the center of the oven and preheat the oven to 375 degrees F. Line two or more cookie sheets with parchment paper.

2. Mix the flour, cinnamon, baking soda, and salt together in a small bowl and set aside for use in Step 4.

3. Place the brown sugar and butter in the bowl of an electric mixer fitted with a paddle attachment. Beat on medium-low speed until well combined. Add the egg, turn the mixer to medium speed, and beat until fluffy, about 1 to 2 minutes. Gradually add the apple cider (or juice) and vanilla extract, and beat well. Scrape down the sides of the bowl as needed to ensure even mixing. (The mixture may separate slightly, especially if the cider is cold, but this is not a problem.)

4. Turn the mixer to low speed and gradually add the dry ingredients, mixing just until incorporated. Stir in the apples, walnuts, dates, and

butterscotch morsels, taking care to evenly distribute the goodies and to break apart any date pieces that may be clinging to one another.

5. Portion the dough into mounds using a level 1⅝-inch (#40) scoop or 1 heaping tablespoon per mound. Place the mounds about 2 inches apart on the prepared cookie sheets. Flatten each mound into a 2-inch disk using the palm of your hand. Lightly dampen your palm as needed to prevent sticking.

6. Bake about 15 minutes, or until golden brown and firm around the edges. (For a plumper cookie, do not flatten the mounds and bake closer to 17 minutes.) Transfer immediately to wire racks using an offset spatula to prevent breakage. Cool completely before glazing or storing.

7. Make the Apple Cider Glaze (optional). If you'd like to generously frost the cookie tops, combine the powdered sugar, lemon juice, and enough apple cider or juice (about 4 tablespoons) to make a thick, spreadable glaze. Whisk or stir vigorously until very smooth. Spread about 1 teaspoon glaze on top of each cookie.

    If you'd rather drizzle the glaze more sparingly, cut the glaze recipe in half and mix as described above. Thin the glaze by stirring in a small amount (1 to 1½ teaspoons) of additional cider. The glaze should flow freely off a fork but still cling to a "test" cookie without running off. Adjust the glaze consistency as needed by adding more cider to thin it or powdered sugar to thicken it.

8. Place the cookies on wire racks set on parchment paper. (The paper will catch any drippings and make for easy cleanup later.) Use a fork, thin-bladed knife, or parchment pastry cone to distribute the glaze over the cookie tops.

9. Let the glaze dry before storing or packaging the cookies for gift-giving.

The Brown(ie)-Noser
Makes 3½ to 4 dozen (1½-inch) squares

Buttering up a teacher, boss, friend, or family member is easy with this super-charged blonde brownie. *Note:* Omit the rum if too adult for kids.

Complexity:	Active Time:	Type:
❷		Bar

Prep Talk: Allow 1 to 2 hours for the bars to cool before glazing and

another 3 to 4 hours for the glaze to chill before cutting. Glazed bars should be stored in the refrigerator. (The glaze is perishable.) Unglazed brownies are better stored at room temperature. Bars will stay fresh longer if kept in the pan, tightly wrapped in foil, and cut to order. For best eating, serve at room temperature within 3 to 5 days.

Caramel Topping
8 ounces caramel candies (about 27 cubes)
¼ cup heavy cream
1 tablespoon unsalted butter

4½ teaspoons all-purpose flour

½ teaspoon pure vanilla extract

Butterscotch Brownies

2½ cups all-purpose flour

2 teaspoons baking powder

3/8 teaspoon salt

1¼ cups (2½ sticks) unsalted butter, chopped into
    tablespoon-size pieces

2¼ cups firmly packed light brown sugar

3 large eggs, room temperature

1½ teaspoons pure vanilla extract

3 tablespoons dark rum (optional)

2 cups pecan halves, toasted and coarsely chopped

Ganache Glaze (optional)

1 recipe Ganache (p. 149), chocolate increased to 1 pound

1. **Make the Caramel Topping.** Unwrap the caramel candies and combine with the cream and butter in a small nonreactive (stainless steel or coated) saucepan. Place over medium heat and cook, stirring regularly to prevent scorching, until the caramels and butter are completely melted and the mixture has boiled. Remove from the heat. Stir in the flour, mixing well to break apart any lumps. Add the vanilla extract and set the topping in a warm place so the caramel stays fluid while you prepare the brownie batter.

2. Position a rack in the center of the oven and preheat the oven to 350 degrees F. Line a 10 x 15 x 2-inch glass baking dish (sometimes called a roasting pan, p. 10) with foil, leaving a 1-inch overhang around the top edge of the pan. Smooth out any big wrinkles in the foil and then lightly coat the foil with nonstick cooking spray.

3. **Mix the Butterscotch Brownies.** Combine the flour, baking powder, and salt together in a medium bowl. Set aside.

    Place the butter in a medium (3-quart) saucepan over low heat. Once the butter has fully melted, remove it from the heat and stir in the brown sugar, mixing until smooth. (*Note:* Don't be

surprised if the butter and sugar do not completely come together at this point; some separation is normal.) Cool a few minutes; then add the eggs one at a time, whisking well after each addition. Add the vanilla extract and rum, if desired. Gradually add the flour mixture, whisking all the while to keep the batter lump free. Stir in the pecans.

   Turn the batter into the prepared pan and level with a small offset spatula. (The batter will be less than 1 inch thick, but it will bake to about twice its original thickness.)

4. Drizzle the caramel topping evenly over the batter. (If the caramel has thickened and is difficult to drizzle, gently reheat it.) Marble the top (and break apart any large caramel blobs) by drawing a spatula through both the topping and the batter in a random pattern.

5. Bake until a cake tester inserted into the center comes out with moist crumbs on it, and the brownie has pulled away from the edges of the pan, about 35 to 40 minutes. Transfer to a wire rack and cool completely in the pan. (Areas that had larger helpings of caramel topping may sink slightly, but don't worry; the ganache will completely cover any holes.)

6. **Prepare and apply the Ganache Glaze (optional).** Make the glaze only after the brownies have completely cooled. Follow the instructions for Ganache, pages 149 and 150, but increase the chocolate to 1 pound.

   While the ganache is fluid, pour it evenly over the brownie. Gently tilt or shake the pan so that the ganache completely coats the brownie top. Cover with foil, taking care to keep it from touching the ganache. Refrigerate 3 to 4 hours, or until the ganache is firm enough to cut cleanly.

7. Remove the brownies from the pan in one block by gently pulling up on the foil overhang. Place directly on a cutting board. Remove all foil and trim any uneven edges before cutting into 1½-inch squares. For the neatest cuts, slice the bars while the ganache is firm and wipe the knife clean with a warm, damp cloth between slices. Serve at room temperature.

Gold Star

Tasting Not

Yummy.

Definitely make

t home!

Gold Star Macaroons

Makes about 2 dozen (1¾-inch) macaroons

Of all the macaroons I've ever tried (and that's a lot), this version gets a big gold star due to additions of cocoa and chocolate chips.

Complexity:	Active Time:	Type:
		Drop; hand-shaped

Prep Talk: Because of their high sugar content, macaroons are especially susceptible to humidity. Package in airtight containers as soon as they've cooled and store at room temperature. For best eating, serve within 1 to 2 days while the exterior is still crisp.

2½ cups lightly packed sweetened coconut flakes, divided

½ pound pure almond paste

6 tablespoons granulated sugar

6 tablespoons powdered sugar

2 tablespoons cake flour

1 tablespoon unsweetened non-alkalized cocoa powder

¼ teaspoon salt

2 large egg whites

⅜ teaspoon coconut extract

1¼ cups miniature chocolate chips, divided

1. Position a rack in the center of the oven and preheat the oven to 325 degrees F. Line two or more cookie sheets with parchment paper.

2. Place 1 cup coconut in the bowl of a food processor fitted with a metal blade. Break the almond paste into small pieces and add to the coconut. Process 1 to 2 minutes, or until the coconut is very finely ground and the dough begins to come together in a large mass. Sift the sugars, cake flour, cocoa powder, and salt together, and add to the coconut-almond mixture. Process to thoroughly combine. Add the egg whites and coconut extract and process just until the mixture forms a sticky mass, about 15 seconds. Stir as needed to ensure even processing.

3. Turn the dough into a bowl and stir in ½ cup coconut flakes and ½ cup chocolate chips.

4. Pour the remaining 1 cup coconut flakes and ¾ cup chocolate chips into a large bowl or cake pan to form a shallow layer, and break apart any coconut pieces that may be clinging together. Toss to evenly mix.

5. Portion the dough into mounds using a level 1½-inch (#50) scoop or 1 level tablespoon per mound. Roll the mounds between your palms to form 1¼-inch balls, dampening your hands as needed to keep the dough from sticking. Drop the balls, a few at a time, into the coconut–chocolate chip mixture and roll to evenly coat.

6. Place the cookies 1 inch apart on the prepared cookie sheets. Bake 25 to 30 minutes, or until the coconut flakes are nutty brown and the cookies have puffed and cracked ever so slightly. To ensure even browning, rotate the cookie sheet about midway through baking. Cool the cookies 1 to 2 minutes on the cookie sheet; then transfer to wire racks to cool completely before storing. (As the cookies cool, they will get crispy on the outside but will stay lusciously soft on the inside.)

No-Hassle, No-Bake Oatmeal Fudge Cookies (lower right) and Brain Teaser (lower left). *Storage Tip:* Though cookies can be mixed and matched in a display or take-home container, it's best not to store them this way long term, as they will quickly absorb each others' flavors.

Brain Teaser

Makes about 2 dozen (1¾-inch) squares

I bet you tell your kids that eating fruits and veggies will improve their IQs, right? Even if they aren't convinced, here's a sure way to slip some carrots, raisins, and pineapple into their diets. But don't be fooled by all the good things—these carrot Congo-bar twists are succulent and rich.

Complexity:

1

Active Time:

Type:

Bar

Prep Talk: Allow about ½ hour for the crust to cool before topping and another 2 hours for the cookies to cool before cutting. (The bars will cut more neatly if completely cooled.) Bars will stay fresh longer if kept in the pan, tightly wrapped in foil, and cut just before serving. For the crunchiest crust, eat within 1 to 2 days. (Because of its high sugar and fruit content, the filling is moist and will soften the crust over time.)

Shortbread Crust

1½ cups all-purpose flour

¼ cup plus 2 tablespoons granulated sugar

½ teaspoon salt

¾ cup (1½ sticks) unsalted butter, softened and cut into tablespoon-size pieces

Carrot "Cake" Topping

2½ tablespoons all-purpose flour

1¼ teaspoons ground cinnamon

1 teaspoon ground ginger

¾ teaspoon ground cloves

½ teaspoon salt

¼ teaspoon baking soda

1 (14-ounce) can (about 1 cup plus 3 tablespoons)
    sweetened condensed milk

¼ cup plus 2 tablespoons packed light brown sugar

2 large eggs

1 large egg yolk

1 teaspoon pure vanilla extract

1½ cups peeled, shredded carrots (about 1½ large carrots,
    4 ounces each)

1½ cups walnut halves, lightly toasted and chopped

1 cup raisins

½ cup dried pineapple pieces, about 1 (3-ounce) bag,
    finely chopped (optional)

¼ cup powdered sugar (for dusting, optional)

1. Position a rack in the center of the oven and preheat the oven to 350 degrees F. Line a 9 x 13 x 2-inch baking pan with foil, leaving a 1-inch overhang around the top edge of the pan. Smooth out any big wrinkles in the foil and then lightly coat the foil with nonstick cooking spray.

2. **Make the Shortbread Crust.** Combine the flour, sugar, and salt in the bowl of a food processor fitted with a metal blade. Add the butter and process until the mixture just clings together in a ball, about 15 to 20 seconds. Pat the crust into an even layer in the prepared pan. (It may not appear as if you have enough dough, but the crust will puff upon cooking.) Generously prick the dough with a fork.

3. Bake the crust 20 to 25 minutes, or until lightly browned and firm to the touch. (Prick the crust again about midway through baking if it appears overly puffed.) Transfer to a wire rack and cool completely before topping, about ½ hour.

4. **Mix the Carrot "Cake" Topping.** Combine the flour, spices, salt, and baking soda in a small bowl and set aside.

    In a large bowl, whisk together the sweetened condensed milk, brown sugar, eggs, egg yolk, and vanilla extract. Beat until well combined. Gradually whisk in the flour mixture, taking care to break apart any lumps. Stir in the carrots, walnuts, raisins, and,

if desired, pineapple. Pour the topping over the cooled crust and evenly distribute the goodies.

5. Bake the bars 35 to 40 minutes, or until the edges are caramel-brown and the top is slightly puffed. Transfer to a wire rack and cool completely before cutting. (For easiest cutting, allow about 2 hours for the bars to fully cool and set.)

6. Remove the bars from the pan in one block by gently pulling up on the foil overhang and place directly on a cutting board. Remove all foil and trim any uneven edges before cutting with a sharp knife into 1¾-inch squares. For the neatest cuts, wipe the knife clean with a warm, damp cloth between slices. Lightly dust with powdered sugar, if desired, just before serving.

No-Hassle, No-Bake Oatmeal Fudge Cookies
Makes about 2½ dozen (2-inch) cookies

Another wise addition to your after-school repertoire, these creamy no-bake cookies go from mixing bowl to mouth in about 30 minutes. *Note:* It is especially important to have all the ingredients measured and prepped before you start mixing. Once you reach Step 3, you will need to add ingredients quickly before the mixture begins to get firm.

Complexity:	Active Time:	Type:
1		Drop

Prep Talk: Though not essential, a candy thermometer is helpful in Step 2. Store in airtight containers at room temperature up to 1 week, or in the refrigerator if you prefer a firmer consistency.

1½ cups granulated sugar

½ cup evaporated milk

½ cup (1 stick) unsalted butter, cut into tablespoon-size pieces

¼ teaspoon salt

½ cup unsweetened non-alkalized cocoa powder, sifted

¾ cup creamy peanut butter
1½ teaspoons pure vanilla extract
2¼ cups quick-cook oats
¾ cup raisins
¾ cup pecan halves, lightly toasted and coarsely chopped

About 2½ dozen pecan halves, lightly toasted (for topping)

1. Line two or more cookie sheets with parchment paper.

2. Combine the sugar, evaporated milk, butter, and salt in a medium (3-quart) nonreactive (stainless steel or coated) saucepan. Place over medium to medium-high heat and bring to a rolling boil, stirring as needed to make sure the butter has completely melted by the time the mixture boils. Boil about 2 minutes longer, or until the syrup just registers 238 to 240 degrees F on a candy thermometer. Stir as needed to keep the mixture from scorching on the bottom of the pan. (Avoid boiling longer than specified, or the resulting mixture will harden very quickly and become crumbly and difficult to scoop.)

3. Remove the pan from the heat and immediately add the cocoa powder, whisking to break apart any lumps. Whisk in the peanut butter and vanilla extract; then stir in the oats, raisins, and pecans. (The mixture should be shiny and loose at this point.)

4. Work quickly to scoop all the dough while it is still loose. (If the dough begins to set as you scoop, the resulting texture of the cookies will be crumbly.) Portion the dough into mounds using a level 1⅝-inch (#40) scoop or 1 heaping tablespoon per mound. Place the mounds about 1 inch apart on the prepared cookie sheets. Top each cookie with a pecan half and press gently to flatten the cookies to about 2 inches in diameter.

5. Freeze the cookies 15 to 20 minutes, or until completely set. (Alternatively, place them on the counter so the kids can watch them turn into fudge. Setting time can vary considerably, depending on the ambient temperature.)

Peanut Butter and Jelly Sandwiches

Makes about 2 dozen (3-inch) sandwiches

This favorite lunch box staple-turned-cookie ranks top in its class.

Complexity:

Active Time:

Type: Rolled; sandwich

Prep Talk: For easiest handling, the dough must be chilled at least 3 hours before rolling and cutting. Store unfilled cookies in airtight containers at room temperature up to 1 week. Once filled, the sandwiches are best eaten within a few days, as the cookies will soften next to the jam.

1½ cups all-purpose flour
½ teaspoon baking soda
½ teaspoon salt
¾ cup creamy peanut butter
½ cup (1 stick) unsalted butter, softened
½ cup firmly packed light brown sugar
⅓ cup granulated sugar
1 large egg
1 teaspoon pure vanilla extract

¾ to 1 cup seedless red raspberry or strawberry jam (for filling)

1. Combine the flour, baking soda, and salt in a small bowl. Set aside for use in Step 2.

2. Place the peanut butter and butter in the bowl of an electric mixer fitted with a paddle attachment and beat on medium speed until well combined. Gradually add the sugars. Turn the mixer to medium-high speed and beat 1 to 2 minutes longer, until light and fluffy. Add the egg and vanilla extract. Mix until well combined. Scrape down the sides of the bowl as needed to ensure even mixing.

    Turn the mixer to low speed and gradually add the dry ingredients, mixing just until incorporated.

3. Divide the dough into two equal portions and flatten each portion into a disk. Wrap each disk tightly in plastic and refrigerate at least 3 hours, or until firm enough to roll without sticking.

4. Position a rack in the center of the oven and preheat the oven to 375 degrees F. Line two or more cookie sheets with parchment paper.

5. Work with one disk of dough at a time. On a lightly floured surface, roll the dough to a 3/16-inch thickness. Cut into squares using a 2 3/4-inch square cookie cutter, and then cut each square along the diagonal into two triangles. (Should the dough get too sticky to easily roll at any point, simply return it to the refrigerator or freezer until it has firmed up. Chill any scraps before re-rolling.)

6. Place the triangles about 1 inch apart on the prepared cookie sheets and bake 10 to 12 minutes, or until golden brown around the edges. Immediately transfer to wire racks using an offset spatula to prevent breakage. Cool completely. Repeat Steps 5 and 6 with the remaining disk of dough.

7. Preheat the broiler. Turn half of the triangles upside down on a cookie sheet and top each with 1½ level teaspoons jam. Spread the jam into an even layer with a small offset spatula, covering the cookie as completely as possible. Place the cookies under the broiler, in the top third of the oven, for 1 to 2 minutes, just until the jam begins to bubble around the cookie edges. Watch carefully, as the jam and any exposed cookie edges can quickly burn.

8. Transfer the cookies to wire racks. While the jam is still warm, top each cookie with another triangle and gently press together. Cool completely before storing. *Note:* As the jam cools, the sandwiches will hold firmly together without sliding. The bottom cookie, which may have softened under the broiler, will also return to its original crisp state.

COOKIE MONSTER

Who says scary can't be sweet? Whether your occasion is Halloween, an October birthday, or simply the appearance of the full moon, this cookie swap is sure to deliver the necessary suspense.

Before the party begins, cast a spell with the invitation. Tiny wooden "coffins" lure guests to peek inside, where two "bloodshot eyes"—truffles in disguise—accompany a tattered slip of paper with the swap's date, place, and time. Continue the party in the same vein with a startling array of sweets, each one costumed to fit the theme. The mere sight of the cookies will get everyone's adrenaline flowing; the tastes of pumpkin, cinnamon, and other seasonal spices will only quicken the pace.

Conjure up even more excitement with imaginative cookie games. For a round of "Bite the Bat," suspend gingerbread bats from above; then blindfold the kids and give each a spin, along with the challenge to bite as many bat wings as they can. Or turn the game into a group crafting project. Set up work stations in a nearby room and show guests how to make striking mobiles and tabletop trees with branches and cookies.

As the party draws to a close, dole out empty apothecary jars or inexpensive trick-or-treat bags and ask guests to pick their poison from among the cookie remains. No matter the container, remember to have plenty on hand—as everyone knows, an overdose of cookies is a great way to go.

Cause to Celebrate:
Halloween, an October birthday or anniversary, All Saints' Day, the full moon, a harvest celebration.

Counterclockwise from upper left, Candy Corn Cookies, Spider Truffles, Chocolate-Nut Cobweb Cookies, Friendly Ghosts, and Great Pumpkin Cookies. Gingerbread also shows up as tombstones, ghosts, a moon, and a bat-infested house. Not pictured: Eye Candy and Witches' Fingers.

WE'LL BE SEEING YOU SOON...

OCTOBER 31st
THE WITCHING HOUR
(THE STROKE OF MIDNIGHT)
405 NEWPORT AVENUE

JUST BRING YOURSELF
AND
THREE BATCHES OF
YOUR SPOOKIEST COOKIE
(THE RECIPE, TOO!)

RSVP

Eye-Catching Invitations *(opposite)*

To make: Stain small plain wood boxes (available in craft stores) by painting them with a mixture of 1 cup water and several drops black and/or brown food coloring. Wipe off the excess stain and let the boxes dry. Create invitations that will fit inside the box lid with adequate room for the truffles. (These invitations are 2 x 5-inch scrolls with the apropos greeting "We'll be seeing you soon.") To create the appearance of a singed and tattered edge, print a heavy black border around the invitation; then carefully rip through the center of the border along its entire length. Fill the boxes with faux Spanish moss, 2 pieces of Eye Candy (p. 114), and the invitation. Hand-deliver the boxes or send them by priority mail since the candy can spoil after 1 or 2 days without refrigeration.

Stand-ins
Like the idea of this invitation, but short on time?

- Use small black paper boxes or bags and bypass the wood boxes and staining.

- Substitute Halloween-themed gift tags for the invitations rather than printing your own.

- Purchase plain white chocolate–dipped truffles from your favorite confectioner and dress them up with "eye candy" at home.

- Substitute store-bought candy of a completely different ilk and choose a corresponding message. Some combinations to consider: "Boo to you" (with marshmallow ghosts); "No squirming out of this party" (with gummy worms); and "We've picked you" (with tiny cream pumpkins).

Left: To make this macabre graveyard, use Cutout Cookie Gingerbread for the small (4- to 5-inch) tombstones. For 3-D or very large 2-D projects, such as the haunted house façade (background and p. 109), sturdier Construction Gingerbread will yield longer-lasting results due to its use of bread flour. *Note:* Outlining is the decorating technique of choice for very precise linear details, such as the bony wings on the bat and the typewriter-quality letters on the tombstones. For technique details, see page 152.

Gingerbread Jaw-Dropper *(far left)*

To make a haunted house façade: Sketch the outline of a house on a piece of 3-ply cardboard and cut along the outline to create a template. Slide a large piece of rolled Construction Gingerbread (p. 146) onto a parchment paper–lined cookie sheet. Set the template on top of the gingerbread and cut along the edge with a sharp paring knife. Remove any unwanted dough from around the façade and save for another use. Bake the façade as directed on page 147. When cool, decorate with Royal Icing, Halloween candy, and other iced cookies. Let the icing dry completely—ideally overnight—and then prop the façade straight up.

Bat-Mobile *(top middle)*

To make: Glue the end of a length of high-strength monofilament fishing line between two bat cookies using thick Royal Icing. Repeat with more cookies, varying the lengths of line. Let the icing dry overnight; then use a glue gun to attach the other end of each line to a tree branch. Tie a long piece of fishing line to the center of the branch and secure this line to a light fixture or a tree. If the mobile does not hang straight, adjust the cookie positions on the branch. (Remember to hang the mobile within biting reach if you intend to play "Bite the Bat," p. 109.)

Tabletop Tree *(bottom right)*

To make: Anchor branches in tall buckets with rocks and affix the bat cookies to the branches as instructed above. Add a festive glow by gluing small (5- to 6-inch) candles to the "tree," using black spray-painted bottle caps as bobeche. Safety precaution: Even though the bottle caps will catch wax drippings, never leave a lit tree unattended or around the kids.

Top right: Take-home cookies are bewitchingly bottled in apothecary jars with personalized labels. To keep recipe transcription from taking up valuable party time, gather the recipes in advance and print them on the back of the labels.

Top middle and bottom right: What a hoot! This fanciful gingerbread owl casts its shadow on a larger plain yellow moon cookie. See page 154 for tips on making cookie compositions using the appliqué technique.

Eye Candy
Makes about 3 dozen (1¼-inch) truffles

Though this creamy bite of chocolate isn't a cookie in the strict sense, its ghoulish attire earns it a (f)rightful place at any Halloween table. *Note:* The truffle filling is infused with the flavors of hot mulled cider, but the spices can be omitted for those who prefer their chocolate straight up.

Complexity:

Active Time:

Type: N/A

Prep Talk: For easiest handling, the ganache should be chilled for 2 to 3 hours before shaping and dipping. Store finished candy tightly covered in the refrigerator up to 1 week.

1 recipe Ganache (p. 149), cream reduced to 1 cup and corn
    syrup omitted
15 whole cloves
4 cinnamon sticks, broken into large pieces
1 tablespoon coarsely grated orange zest
¼ teaspoon ground cinnamon

1½ pounds premium white chocolate, melted (for dipping)
A few drops red soft gel food coloring (optional, p. 152)

Decoration
½ recipe Royal Icing (p. 151)
35 to 40 drops black soft gel food coloring, or to desired shade
About 1 teaspoon water (to thin the icing)
Assorted candies (for decorating the "eyes;" black string licorice
    and fruit leather work well for "eyebrows" and "eyelashes," whereas
    colorful disk-shaped candies make great "eyeballs")

1. Prepare 1 recipe Ganache as instructed on pages 149 and 150, except reduce the cream to 1 cup and omit the corn syrup. At the end of Step 2, add the whole cloves, cinnamon sticks, and orange zest to the warm cream; then steep about 30 minutes. Reheat the cream before proceeding to Step 3 (p. 150). (*Note:* The spices and zest will be strained out in this step.) Add the ground cinnamon once the chocolate has completely melted and the ganache is smooth.

2. Pour the ganache into a shallow pan to a ½- to ¾-inch depth. Cover and chill 2 to 3 hours, or until firm enough to be rolled into balls without melting or misshaping in your hands. (If the ganache cannot be easily and smoothly rolled, let it soften at room temperature until it reaches a workable consistency.)

3. Line two cookie sheets with parchment paper. Using a 1-inch melon baller, scoop the ganache into ¾- to 1-inch balls. Roll the balls between your palms to make them perfectly round and set on the prepared cookie sheets. (If the chocolate melts in your hands, cool them by rinsing under cold water. If the ganache is still sloppy, return it to the refrigerator for further chilling.) Cover and refrigerate the balls until ready to decorate.

4. Dip the truffles. Pour the melted white chocolate into a small bowl or measuring cup to a 3- to 4-inch depth. Work with one sheet of truffles at a time, keeping the other one in the refrigerator as you work.

    Place a truffle on a chocolate dipping fork or a table fork and submerge it completely in the white chocolate. Gently shake off any excess chocolate and then wipe the truffle bottom clean by dragging it along the edge of the bowl. (This will prevent a "foot" of chocolate from pooling around the candy.) Return the truffle to the cookie sheet. (If the white chocolate is sullied with melted truffle filling, your white chocolate is too hot. Scoop out any traces of dark chocolate and let the chocolate cool slightly before you dip again.)

5. (Optional) To create a "bloodshot eye," work quickly before the chocolate sets. Dip the tip of a toothpick or cake tester into red food coloring and gently draw the toothpick through the chocolate to create a marbled effect.

6. Repeat Steps 4 to 5 with the remaining truffles on the first cookie sheet and refrigerate 10 to 15 minutes to allow the chocolate to set. Do not allow the truffles to sit for an extended period at room temperature, or the chocolate can turn dull and streaky.

7. Repeat Steps 4 to 6 with the truffles on the second cookie sheet.

8. Decorate. Prepare ½ recipe Royal Icing. Portion out half of the icing, add the black food coloring, and mix well. Thin with water (about 1 teaspoon) until the icing is the desired consistency for beadwork (p. 152). Fill a parchment paper cone with the black icing and another cone with the remaining white icing. Cut a small (⅛-inch) hole in the tip of each cone.

   Using the white icing, affix assorted candies onto the truffles to create eyeballs, brows, and lashes. Add "pupils" by piping a small dot of black Royal Icing in the center of each eyeball.

Variation: Spider Truffles

1. Cut black licorice strings into 1¾- to 2-inch pieces, allotting 6 to 8 pieces per truffle. Bend each piece into a half circle and set aside. (Or use licorice strings that come wound into a disk. Once unwound, they will form perfect arcs.)

2. Replace the white chocolate with semisweet chocolate in Step 4 (p. 114). Dip the truffles as instructed.

3. Before the chocolate sets, gently press the licorice strings into the sides of each truffle to form the "spider legs." (Each licorice string should stand upright in an arc.) You can also insert a pair of white jimmies for "fangs," if desired. Refrigerate 10 to 15 minutes to allow the chocolate to set.

4. Add two eyeballs to each spider using tiny candies and Royal Icing as instructed in Step 8, above.

Chocolate-Nut Cobweb Cookies

Makes about 2 ½ dozen (2 ¾- to 3-inch) cookies

This cookie is the very same chocolate-nut wafer that was the cornerstone of Usher family snacks throughout the years. However, here it is dressed for the occasion in a showy icing cobweb. *Note:* Increase the salt from ¾ teaspoon to 1 teaspoon if you plan to do the optional decorating with sugar. Trust me—the interplay of salt and sugar is incredibly addictive.

Complexity:

1

Active Time:

Type:

Drop; hand-shaped

Prep Talk: Store in airtight containers at room temperature up to 1 week.

¾ cup all-purpose flour
¾ to 1 teaspoon salt
1 ¼ cups granulated sugar, divided
½ cup butter-flavored shortening
1 large egg
1 teaspoon pure vanilla extract
2 ounces premium unsweetened chocolate, melted and cooled
1 cup walnut halves, lightly toasted and finely chopped

1 tablespoon vegetable oil (for greasing glass)

Decoration (optional)
½ recipe Royal Icing (p. 151), thinned for outlining (p. 152)
About ½ cup granulated sugar (for sifting)

1. Position a rack in the center of the oven and preheat the oven to 375 degrees F. Line two or more cookie sheets with parchment paper.

2. Combine the flour and salt together in a small bowl and set aside for use in Step 4.

3. Place 1 cup sugar and the shortening in the bowl of an electric mixer fitted with a paddle attachment and beat on medium-low speed until well combined. Add the egg and vanilla extract; turn the mixer to medium speed and beat until light and fluffy, about 1 to 2 minutes. Add the melted chocolate (it should be cool but not set) and continue to beat until the mixture is uniformly blended. Scrape down the sides of the bowl as needed to ensure even mixing.

4. Turn the mixer to low speed and gradually add the flour mixture, mixing just until combined. Stir in the walnuts.

5. Roll the dough between your palms into 1 ¼-inch balls. For the most uniform balls, first portion the dough into mounds using a level 1 ½-inch (#50) scoop or 1 level tablespoon per mound; then roll into perfect balls. Place the balls 2 to 3 inches apart on the prepared cookie sheets.

6. Flatten the balls into 2 ¼- to 2 ½-inch disks with the bottom of a lightly greased glass dipped in the remaining sugar. To prevent sticking, make sure the glass bottom is thoroughly coated with sugar before each press. After every few presses, clean off the excess sugar that accumulates around the bottom edge of the glass.

7. Bake 7 to 9 minutes, or until dry on top and firm to the touch. Cool 1 to 2 minutes on the pan; then transfer to wire racks and cool completely before decorating or storing.

8. Decorate (optional). Fill a parchment pastry cone with Royal Icing, thinned for outlining (p. 152), and cut a very small hole (less than ¹⁄₁₆ inch diameter) in the tip. Place about ½ cup sugar in a sieve over a large bowl.
   Work with one cookie at a time. Pipe a delicate Royal Icing cobweb on the back of the cookie and immediately sift sugar over the top. Shake the excess sugar off the cookie and into the bowl so it can be re-used on the other cookies. Repeat with the remaining cookies. Let the icing dry before storing.
   Note: There will be leftover Royal Icing. Cover and store as directed (p. 151) for another use.

Witches' Fingers

Makes about 6 dozen (4-inch) "fingers"

You needn't have a steady hand or any advanced decorating skill to make these crunchy cookie fingers. In fact, a few intentional "wrinkles" and "warts" will only enhance their deliciously creepy effect.

Complexity:

Active Time:

Type: Pressed or hand-shaped

Prep Talk: Store in airtight containers at room temperature up to 2 weeks.

2½ cups all-purpose flour
2 teaspoons ground cinnamon
¾ teaspoon salt
1 cup (1 stick) butter-flavored shortening
1 (3-ounce) package cream cheese, room temperature
¾ cup granulated sugar
¼ cup firmly packed light brown sugar
1 large egg yolk
1¼ teaspoons maple extract, or to taste
1 teaspoon pure vanilla extract

About ¼ cup sliced almonds (1 per cookie, for the "nails")

1. Position a rack in the center of the oven and preheat the oven to 350 degrees F. Line two or more cookie sheets with parchment paper.

2. Combine the flour, cinnamon, and salt in a small bowl. Set aside for use in Step 4.

3. Place the shortening and cream cheese in the bowl of an electric mixer fitted with a paddle attachment and beat on medium speed until smooth. Gradually add the sugars and beat 1 to 2 minutes longer, or until light and fluffy. Add the egg yolk and extracts, and mix until well combined. Scrape down the sides of the bowl as needed to ensure even mixing.

4. Turn the mixer to low speed and gradually add the dry ingredients, mixing just until combined.

5. Fill a cookie press with the dough and fit the end of the press with a ¼- to ⅜-inch round pastry tip. Cover any dough that is not in use with plastic wrap to keep it from drying out. (*Note:* Piping through a traditional pastry bag is possible, but because the dough is firm, this approach will require a lot of force. To avoid hand fatigue, a cookie press is a far better option. If you don't own a cookie press, the dough may be hand-shaped by rolling it into cylinders and following the other shaping instructions in Step 6.)

6. Press the dough onto the prepared cookie sheets into ⅜-inch-diameter cylinders, each about 3½ inches long. For the most lifelike fingers, pipe the cookies no more than two-thirds the width of an actual adult finger, as the dough will spread during baking. Should the dough break while you are pressing, no worries. Simply pinch the pieces together into one finger. Remember: In this case, gnarly is better than neat. Apply varying pressure as you pipe to create wrinkled "knuckles." If desired, score deeper wrinkles into the knuckles with a paring knife, taking care not to cut completely through the cookies.

7. Press a sliced almond into one end of each cookie to make the "nail."

8. Bake 10 to 12 minutes, or until very lightly browned. About midway through baking, press any almonds that have shifted back into place. While the cookies are hot from the oven, gently push in the sides to make the fingers more three-dimensional. (The cookies will spread and flatten a little during baking.) Let the fingers cool on the cookie sheets until they can be easily moved without breaking, about 3 to 5 minutes. Carefully transfer to wire racks with an offset spatula and cool completely before storing.

Great Pumpkin Cookies

Makes 2½ to 3 dozen (2-inch) "pumpkins"

Embellished with orange glaze, cinnamon stick "stems," and green sugar "vines," these pumpkins appear to be freshly plucked from the patch. *Note:* For smoother pumpkins for decorating, you may decrease or omit the raisins and walnuts. Without these add-ins, the recipe yields closer to 2½ dozen cookies.

Complexity: **1**

Active Time:

Type: Drop

Prep Talk: Store in airtight containers at room temperature up to 5 days. Because of their high pumpkin content, these soft cookies will get even softer within a few days, especially under humid conditions. Eat freshly baked if you want to enjoy a crunchy exterior.

Pumpkin Spice Cookies

2¼ cups all-purpose flour
2 tablespoons cornstarch
1 teaspoon baking soda
1 teaspoon baking powder
2½ teaspoons ground cinnamon
1 teaspoon ground cloves
1 teaspoon freshly grated nutmeg
¾ teaspoon ground ginger
¾ teaspoon salt
1 cup granulated sugar
¾ cup firmly packed light brown sugar
½ cup (1 stick) plus 2 tablespoons unsalted butter, softened
1 large egg
1¼ cups canned pure pumpkin purée (with no added sugar or spices)
1½ teaspoons pure vanilla extract
1½ cups walnut halves, lightly toasted, cooled, and coarsely chopped (optional)
1⅓ cups raisins (optional)

Orange Icing and Glaze (optional)

1 recipe Royal Icing (p. 151)

½ to 1 teaspoon water (to thin the icing)
About 60 drops orange soft gel food coloring (p. 152)
½ teaspoon pure orange extract
About 3 drops red soft gel food coloring
About 3 drops brown soft gel food coloring
About 4 tablespoons strained freshly squeezed orange juice
Powdered sugar (as needed to thicken glaze)

Decoration (optional)

About 12 cinnamon sticks, cut into 2½ to 3 dozen small (¾- to 1-inch) pieces (1 per cookie)
2½ to 3 dozen (¾- to 1-inch) fondant leaves (1 per cookie, see "Fun with Fondant," p. 155)
2½ to 3 dozen (1½- to 2-inch) fondant vines (1 per cookie, see "Fun with Fondant," p. 155)

1. Position a rack in the center of the oven and preheat the oven to 350 degrees F. Line two or more cookie sheets with parchment paper.

2. Mix the Pumpkin Spice Cookies. Combine the flour, cornstarch, baking soda, baking powder, spices, and salt in a bowl. Set aside.

   Place the sugars and butter in the bowl of an electric mixer fitted with a paddle attachment and beat on medium-low speed until well combined. Add the egg and beat on medium-high speed until light and fluffy, about 1 to 2 minutes. Turn the mixer to low speed and beat in the pumpkin purée and vanilla extract. Scrape down the sides of the bowl as needed to ensure even mixing. *Note:* The batter will separate slightly after the addition of the pumpkin, but this is completely expected.

   Stir in the flour mixture, followed by the walnuts and raisins, if desired.

3. Portion the dough into mounds using a level 1⅝-inch (#40) scoop or 1 heaping tablespoon per mound. Place the mounds about 2 inches apart on the prepared cookie sheets. (A scoop will make rounder pumpkins than a tablespoon.)

4. Bake 20 to 25 minutes, or until dry and firm on the outside and

lightly browned on the bottom. Immediately transfer to wire racks and cool completely before storing or glazing.

5. **Mix the Orange Icing and Glaze (optional).** Prepare 1 recipe Royal Icing. Portion out ½ cup. Add enough water (½ to 1 teaspoon) to bring this portion to outlining consistency (p. 152). Stir in a drop of orange food coloring to make a pale shade. Cover the surface of the icing flush with plastic wrap and set aside for use in Step 7.

 To the remaining icing, add the orange extract and the rest of the orange food coloring, and mix until well combined. To enrich the bright orange to a burnished shade, add the red and brown food coloring, if desired. Gradually add enough orange juice to make a thick glaze. (The glaze should thinly coat a "test" cookie, but you should not be able to see through it. Adjust the glaze consistency as needed by adding more juice to thin it or powdered sugar to thicken it.)

6. **Apply the glaze and cinnamon sticks (optional).** Set a wire rack over a sheet of parchment paper. (The paper will catch the glaze drippings and make for easier cleanup later.)

 Work with one cookie at a time. Hold the cookie by the bottom and completely immerse its top in the dark orange glaze. Turn the cookie right side up and gently shake it to remove excess glaze and to smooth the top. Place on the rack and insert a small piece of cinnamon stick into the top center of the cookie to make the pumpkin stem. Repeat with the remaining cookies. (Remember: Tell guests to remove the cinnamon sticks before eating.)

 Before the glaze dries, slide a paring knife under each cookie to sever any drippings that may be clinging to the rack. (The glaze will otherwise dry onto the rack, making it more difficult to remove the cookies later.) Let the cookies dry until the glaze loses its sheen.

7. **Add contours; decorate with fondant leaves and vines (optional).** Fill a parchment paper cone with the reserved pale orange icing and cut a small (⅛-inch or less) hole in the tip. Add contours to the pumpkins by piping 8 to 9 thin lines radiating out from the cinnamon stick stem on each cookie. For the finishing touch, use the icing to glue a fondant leaf and vine around each stem.

8. Let the glaze (and any pumpkin contours) dry completely before storing.

 Note: There will be leftover Royal Icing. Cover and store as directed (p. 151) for another use.

Candy Corn Cookies
Makes about 1½ dozen (3-inch) triangles

A touch of natural cinnamon or orange extract adds the seasonal spice to this styling variation of Classic Icebox Cookie Dough.

Complexity:	Active Time:	Type:
		Hand-shaped; rolled; icebox

Prep Talk: For best results, the dough must be chilled for 1 to 2 hours before shaping and then for another 1 to 2 hours before slicing—so plan accordingly. Shaped dough can be stored in the freezer up to 1 month with minimal loss of flavor if tightly wrapped in plastic and then foil. When you're ready for cookies, simply slice and bake. Store baked cookies in airtight containers up to 5 days. For the crunchiest eating, enjoy within 24 hours.

1 recipe Classic Icebox Cookie Dough (p. 144), less ¼ teaspoon baking soda
2 teaspoons natural cinnamon or orange extract, or other clear flavoring (p. 156)
About 34 to 35 drops orange soft gel food coloring (p. 152)
About 2 drops red soft gel food coloring (optional)
About 10 to 11 drops yellow soft gel food coloring

1. Prepare 1 recipe Classic Icebox Cookie Dough through Step 3 (p. 144), but reduce the baking soda by ¼ teaspoon and add the cinnamon, orange, or other clear extract along with the vanilla extract. (*Note:* Dark extracts like black walnut and maple are also wonderful, especially in the fall. However, use them more sparingly—unless you don't mind tinting the dough.)

2. Divide the dough into two equal portions.

3. Combine the first half of the dough with one-quarter of the second half. Add enough orange food coloring to the combined mass to make a bright orange shade. Mix well to evenly distribute the color. Intensify the orange color by adding the red food coloring, if desired. Mix well.

4. Divide the remaining dough into two portions, one about three times the size of the other. To the larger portion, add enough yellow food coloring to make a bright yellow shade and mix well. Leave the smaller portion as-is.

5. Flatten the three colors of dough into separate disks and wrap each disk tightly in plastic. Refrigerate 1 to 2 hours before shaping in Steps 6 to 7, below.

6. On a lightly floured surface, shape the yellow dough into a 3½ x 4½-inch rectangle, about ½ to ¾ inch thick. Shape the orange dough into a 3½ x 4½-inch rectangle, about 1½ to 1¾ inches thick. Lightly brush the top of the yellow rectangle with egg wash (p. 144) and set the orange rectangle on top. Gently press the two rectangles together.

7. Shape the remaining white dough into a 1 x 4½-inch rectangle, about ½ to ¾ inch thick, and affix it to the top center of the orange dough with egg wash. The resulting log should be about 2¾ inches tall at the highest point, with a cross section that completely fills a 3¼-inch triangle cookie cutter (see photo above).

8. Wrap the log in plastic and freeze 1 to 2 hours, or until quite firm and easily sliced without misshaping. (Don't worry about the irregular edges; they will be trimmed in the next step.)

9. Cut the log crosswise into ³/₁₆-inch-thick slices. Cut each slice into a triangle using a 3¼-inch triangle cookie cutter, taking care to lop off the uneven edges of the log.

10. Transfer the triangles to parchment paper–lined cookies sheets. To mimic candy corn as closely as possible, trim two opposing sides of each triangle to make it narrower; then blunt the triangle corners by gently patting them with your fingertip. Bake and cool as indicated on page 144. *Note:* Be sure to bake the scraps as well. Though they won't look like candy corn, they will be tasty.

Friendly Ghosts

Makes about 2 dozen
(1¾ x 2¼- to 2½-inch-tall) "ghosts"

Enshrouded in meringue, these chewy date and nut treats are oh-so-sweet. *Note:* For a quick and more kid-friendly option, omit the filling.

Complexity:

2

Active Time:

Type:

Drop; hand-shaped;
piped

Prep Talk: Because meringue quickly attracts moisture, package these cookies in airtight containers as soon as they've cooled. Store at room temperature up to 1 week. Even if properly stored, the cookies may still get sticky due to their high fruit content. In this case, re-dry in a 225 degree F oven, if desired.

Date-Nut Filling

1 cup dried pitted dates (stems removed), finely chopped
1½ teaspoons finely grated orange zest

3 tablespoons freshly squeezed orange juice

2 tablespoons candied orange peel, finely chopped

1½ tablespoons Grand Marnier or other premium orange liqueur

½ cup plus 2 tablespoons pecan halves, toasted and finely chopped

¾ teaspoon ground cinnamon

⅜ teaspoon ground cloves

Meringue Cloak

4 large egg whites, room temperature

¼ teaspoon cream of tartar

1 cup sifted superfine sugar

1½ teaspoons cornstarch

About ½ tablespoon miniature chocolate chips (or about 4 dozen chips, 2 per cookie, for the "eyes")

1. Position a rack in the center of the oven and preheat the oven to 225 degrees F. Line two cookie sheets with parchment paper. (If you have two ovens, preheat both. The meringue needs to be baked immediately or it softens and deflates. The cookies will also dry more evenly with one cookie sheet per oven. If you don't have two ovens, you'll need to make a second batch of meringue to coat the cookies on the second cookie sheet. But do so only after the first sheet is out of the oven.)

2. Mix the Date-Nut Filling. Combine the dates, orange zest, juice, peel, and liqueur in a medium (3-quart) nonreactive (stainless steel or coated) saucepan. Cook over medium heat, stirring regularly, until the dates have softened and all of the liquid has been absorbed, about 10 minutes. Cook the mixture another 3 to 5 minutes to dry it further. Stir regularly to prevent scorching. Remove from the heat and stir in the chopped pecans and spices. Cool the mixture completely before shaping.

3. Portion the filling into small mounds using a level 1- to 1⅛-inch (#100) scoop or 1 level teaspoon per mound. Roll the mounds between your palms to form uniform ¾-inch balls and arrange them evenly around the perimeter of each cookie sheet. (It will be

easier to add the chocolate chip eyes to the cookies in Step 6 if the cookies are arranged this way.)

4. Mix the Meringue Cloak. Place the egg whites and cream of tartar in the clean bowl of an electric mixer fitted with a whip attachment. (*Note:* Be sure the whites are at room temperature, as cold meringue is more likely to crack in the heat of the oven. The bowl, whip attachment, and all mixing utensils should also be completely free of fat, or the egg whites will not stiffen.) Beat on low speed until the whites are frothy. Turn the mixer to medium speed and gradually add the superfine sugar, no more than 1 tablespoon at a time. Quickly scrape down the sides of the bowl and then turn the mixer to high speed. Continue beating until the whites are very stiff and glossy and the sugar has completely dissolved, about 10 minutes. Sprinkle the cornstarch evenly over the top and beat until incorporated, about 30 seconds longer.

5. Fit a pastry bag with a large (¾-inch) 8- to 10-pronged star tip and fill with meringue. Work on one cookie at a time, but work quickly before the meringue deflates. Hold the bag perpendicular to the date ball with the pastry tip directly touching the top, and press so the meringue covers as much of the ball as possible. Slowly lift the pastry bag straight up, still applying pressure, to make a ghost that stands 2¼ to 2½ inches tall; then pull up quickly, without applying pressure, to create a peak. Repeat with the remaining meringue.

6. For the ghosts' eyes, carefully place two mini chocolate chips on the side of each cookie, about one-third of the way from the cookie top. (Insert the tips of the chocolate chips into the meringue so that the round bottoms are left exposed.) Gently press the chips into the meringue with the tip of a paring knife.

7. Bake until bone-dry to the touch but only minimally discolored, about 1½ to 2 hours. (*Note:* Drying time varies significantly with ambient humidity. Bake toward the longer end of the spectrum on rainy days.) Immediately transfer to a wire rack and cool completely before storing.

DECK THE HALLS

'Tis the season to be jolly. Yet 'tis also the time for whirlwind entertaining. If you're hosting a swap this season, it's more important than ever to express your gratitude for the work guests will do. Pats on the back are great, of course, but a party full of distinctive touches is an even better present to give in return.

Take this swap's thoughtful lead as an example. To help guests with the season's baking, the party details and recipes are ironed onto dish towels to make novel—and useful—invitations. At the front door, guests are welcomed with a gingerbread wreath bearing a message of yuletide joy. Inside, the cookie table shimmers in soft green and gold, setting off a dramatic centerpiece of sugar cookie "trees"—star-shaped cutouts stacked high on candlesticks. Surrounding this enchanted forest is a luscious terrain of rock candy and cookie snowballs, frosted lavishly with powdered sugar. Gingerbread snowflakes, glittering with edible gold powder and beads, descend in a flurry from overhead, while scattered gingerbread votives complete the cookie look by warming up the wintry scene.

The holiday baking theme continues through to the final favor. Pastry blenders outfitted with cookie recipes are presented to guests on an antique wire dish rack. What guests can't take in at the party, they fortunately get to take home. Gingerbread boxes filled with surplus cookies extend the pleasure of this rare and memorable holiday gift.

Cause to Celebrate:
Christmas; Hanukkah; a winter anniversary, wedding, or birthday; to beat the winter doldrums; to ring in the New Year.

Counterclockwise from upper left, Chocolate–Peanut Butter Yule Logs, Cranberry-Pistachio Biscotti, Gingersnap Thumbprints with Cranberry-Apricot Filling, Eggnog Cheesecake Streusel Bars, Golden Fruitcake Nuggets, Hot Buttered Rum Meltaways (center), and anise-scented sugar cookie "trees." Not pictured: Cocoa-Date Fruitcake Nuggets. (See page 149 for the anise variation of Signature Sugar Cookie Dough.)

Dish Towel Invitations

To make: Digitally scan gift wrap and/or vintage holi-day postcards and then print them onto iron-on transfer paper (available in most office supply and craft stores) along with the invitation and some favorite cookie recipes. Follow the ironing instructions on the transfer paper package label. *Note:* Iron-on transfers will take best to light-colored fabrics with minimal texture, such as tightly woven cotton. Also, remember to reverse your image so it reads in the right direction after it is ironed on.

Stand-in

• If not a dish towel as an invitation, then why not an apron to fit this party's baking theme? Add pockets where needed and tuck printed invitations inside them, or pin the invitations in place. Wrap the aprons in boxes before dropping them in the mail.

A Sweet Welcome Wreath

To make: Cut a large (9½ x 13-inch) oval (or circle) from Construction Gingerbread (p. 146), using an oval (or round) cake pan as your cutting guide. Before baking, use a ⅜- to ½-inch round pastry tip to cut two holes at the top of the oval, about 6 to 7 inches apart. Bake and cool the gingerbread as directed on page 147. Use thick Royal Icing to attach decorated snowflake cookies around the edge and a yuletide greeting, spelled out with cookie letters, in the middle. Once the icing is dry, thread the holes with ribbon and hang your creation. Avoid hanging with wire or string, as they can sometimes cut through the wreath. For tips on cutting and baking large gingerbread pieces and working with Royal Icing, see pages 147 and 151, respectively.

Opposite: Uniquely fragrant, flavorful, and showy, cutout cookies make a grander sensory statement than any other party prop I know. At this swap, they're used for votive candle holders and snowflake ornaments that hang from an ornate chandelier, as well as for "trees" in the forest centerpiece (p. 126).

Bottom right: Clear glass ornaments filled with rock candy, gold sugar beads, snippets of tinsel, and cookie names identify this swap's treats.

Holiday Card Recipe Collections

To make: Digitally scan vintage holiday postcards (or modern-day cards) and print the images onto card-stock, along with the party's recipes on the back. Trim the cards to the same size, insert an eyelet into the corner of each card, and then bind the collections with gold wire, handmade gift tags, and/or mercury glass beads from old Christmas garlands. Slip the collections into a pastry blender and give both as gifts.

Bottom right: Dressed up with gold luster dust, iced gingerbread snowflakes out-shimmer even the showiest cookie. When applied dry, the dust casts a subtle glow (background of top cookie). When mixed with extract and painted on wet, it imparts a more obvious luster (bottom cookie, details on top). For luster dust sources, see page 156; for dusting and painting techniques, see pages 153 and 154.

Top left: There's no reason to take holiday leftovers home on ho-hum paper plates—especially when Construction Gingerbread and Royal Icing are easily turned into tasty cookie boxes. See page 148 for tips on gingerbread box construction.

Stand-Ins
Some easy no-bake take-home container options . . .

- Vintage ornament boxes lined with tissue paper or gift wrap (pictured above; Cocoa-Date Fruitcake Nuggets, center)

- Inexpensive Christmas stockings labeled with guests' names and plumped with leftovers placed first in plastic bags

- Wrapped gift boxes personalized with gift tags bearing guests' names

131

Eggnog Cheesecake Streusel Bars

Makes about 2 dozen (1¾-inch) squares

Spiked with the familiar flavors of eggnog and loaded with buttery cocoa streusel, this luscious cheesecake-cookie is guaranteed to draw big crowds. *Note:* Never substitute pre-ground nutmeg for freshly grated, as the former can be harsh and bitter. For a plain vanilla version for kids, omit the grated nutmeg, bourbon, and rum extract in the cheesecake and increase the vanilla extract to 2 teaspoons.

Complexity: **1**

Active Time:

Type: Bar

Prep Talk: For easiest cutting, chill at least 2 hours before slicing. Because the bars are perishable, they must be stored in the fridge. Bars will stay fresh longer if kept in the pan, tightly wrapped in foil, and cut just before serving. For best flavor and texture, serve at room temperature within 2 to 3 days, before the streusel softens.

Cocoa Streusel Crust (and Topping)

2 cups plus 3 tablespoons all-purpose flour, divided

1 cup plus 3 tablespoons firmly packed light brown sugar, divided

4 tablespoons unsweetened non-alkalized cocoa powder, divided

¼ teaspoon salt

1 cup (2 sticks) plus 3 tablespoons unsalted butter, softened and divided

1 teaspoon freshly grated nutmeg

Eggnog Cheesecake Filling

2 (8-ounce) packages cream cheese, room temperature

½ cup plus 2 tablespoons granulated sugar

2 large eggs, room temperature

2½ teaspoons bourbon

1½ teaspoons freshly grated nutmeg, or to taste

1 teaspoon rum extract

1 teaspoon pure vanilla extract

½ cup premium milk chocolate chips (for topping)

1¼ cups pecan halves, lightly toasted, cooled, and coarsely chopped (for topping)

Caramel Drizzle (optional)

4 ounces caramel candies (about 14 cubes)

2 tablespoons heavy cream

½ tablespoon unsalted butter

1. Position a rack in the center of the oven and preheat the oven to 350 degrees F. Line a 9 x 13 x 2-inch baking pan with foil, leaving a 1-inch overhang around the top edge of the pan. Smooth out any big wrinkles in the foil; then lightly coat the foil with nonstick cooking spray.

2. Mix the Cocoa Streusel Crust. In a medium bowl, combine 1¼ cups plus 3 tablespoons flour, ¼ cup plus 3 tablespoons brown sugar, 2 tablespoons cocoa powder, and the salt. Using a fork or your hands, thoroughly work in ¾ cup plus 1 tablespoon butter until you have a moist dough. (There should be no dry spots.) Press the dough firmly into an even layer in the bottom of the pan. Prick generously with a fork.

3. Bake the crust about 15 minutes, or until set but still soft. (The top will look dull and ever so slightly puffed.) Transfer to a wire rack and cool completely before filling.

4. Make the Cocoa Streusel Topping. Combine the remaining ¾ cup flour, ¾ cup brown sugar, 2 tablespoons cocoa powder, and nutmeg in a small bowl. Work in the remaining 6 tablespoons butter until the dry ingredients are uniformly moistened. (The mixture will be crumbly, but there should be no dry spots.) Set aside for use in Step 6.

5. Mix the Eggnog Cheesecake Filling. Place the cream cheese in the bowl of an electric mixer fitted with a paddle attachment. Beat on medium speed until smooth and creamy, less than 1 minute. Gradually add the sugar and continue to beat until the sugar has dissolved, about 1 minute. (You should feel no grit when you smear a bit of batter between your fingers.) Add the eggs one at a time, beating well after each addition. To keep the batter completely smooth, scrape down the sides of the bowl regularly.

   Turn the mixer to low speed and add the bourbon, nutmeg, and extracts. Mix until well blended.

6. Pour the filling onto the cooled crust and spread into an even layer. Sprinkle the streusel topping evenly over the filling, followed by the chocolate chips and pecans. Gently press the toppings into the cheesecake.

7. Bake the cheesecake about 30 minutes, or until slightly puffed and firm through to the center. Transfer to a wire rack to cool completely.

8. Prepare the Caramel Drizzle (optional). Unwrap the caramel candies and combine them with the cream and butter in a small nonreactive (stainless steel or coated) saucepan. Set over medium-low heat and stir regularly until the caramels are melted and the mixture is well blended. Drizzle 3 to 4 tablespoons over the top of the cheesecake.

9. Cover the pan and refrigerate at least 2 hours.

10. Remove the cheesecake from the pan in one block by gently pulling up on the foil overhang or by easing the block out with an offset spatula. Place directly on a cutting board and remove all foil. Trim any uneven edges before cutting the block into 1¾-inch squares. For the neatest cuts, use a sharp knife, wiped clean with a warm, damp cloth between slices. (If the chocolate chips are difficult to cut, heat the knife blade directly over a hot burner before cutting.)

Gingersnap Thumbprints with Cranberry-Apricot Filling

Makes 3½ to 4 dozen (1¾-inch) thumbprints

This cookie is doubly delectable, as it combines two holiday must-haves—the classic thumbprint and the gingersnap.

Complexity:

Active Time:

Type: Drop; hand-shaped

Prep Talk: Store in airtight containers at room temperature up to 1 week. For the firmest texture, enjoy within the first 3 days.

Cranberry-Apricot Filling

¾ cup apricot jam
⅓ cup dried cranberries, finely chopped

Gingersnap Thumbprints

2 cups all-purpose flour
2 teaspoons ground ginger
1½ teaspoons ground cinnamon
½ teaspoon ground cloves
¼ teaspoon salt
⅓ cup minced crystallized ginger
1 cup (2 sticks) unsalted butter, slightly softened
½ cup granulated sugar
1 tablespoon mild molasses
2 large eggs, separated
1 teaspoon pure vanilla extract

1¾ cups slivered almonds, finely chopped (for rolling)

1. Position a rack in the center of the oven and preheat the oven to 350 degrees F. Line two or more cookie sheets with parchment paper.

2. **Make the Cranberry-Apricot Filling.** Place the jam in a small bowl. If there are any large (greater than ½-inch) chunks of apricot in the jam, pull them out and chop them into small pieces. Stir the pieces back into the jam along with the cranberries. Set aside for use in Step 8.

3. **Mix the Gingersnap Thumbprints.** Mix the flour, spices, and salt together in a medium bowl. Stir in the crystallized ginger, taking care to break apart any pieces that may be clinging to one another. Set aside.

   Place the butter and sugar in the bowl of an electric mixer fitted with a paddle attachment. Beat on medium speed until light and fluffy, about 1 to 2 minutes. Add the molasses, egg yolks, and vanilla extract, and beat until well blended. Scrape down the sides of the bowl as needed to ensure even mixing. Turn the mixer to low speed and gradually add the flour mixture, blending just until incorporated.

4. Place the chopped almonds in a large bowl or cake pan to form a shallow layer. Lightly beat the egg whites and set aside for use in Step 6.

5. Roll the dough between your palms into 1-inch balls. For the most uniform balls, first portion the dough into 1-inch mounds using a level 1⅜-inch (#70) scoop or 2 level teaspoons per mound; then roll into perfect balls. If the butter was overly soft to start, the dough may be sticky and hard to handle. Chill as needed until easily shaped. Take care not to overchill, however, or the dough may crack when you make the indentations in Step 7.

6. Work with one ball at a time. Lightly coat it with beaten egg white and then tumble in the almonds to evenly coat. Roll between your palms again to firmly fix the nuts in place. Repeat with the remaining balls.

7. Arrange the cookies 1 to 2 inches apart on the prepared cookie sheets. Using your thumb or the end of a round-handled spoon, make a deep cup-shaped indentation in the center of each cookie.

8. Bake the cookies 13 to 14 minutes, or until the nuts are lightly browned. Remove from the oven and re-press each indentation. Fill each indentation with 1 rounded ½ teaspoon filling and then bake another 3 to 4 minutes. (*Note:* Do not overfill or the jam may spill out of the cookie as it heats up.) Using an offset spatula to prevent breakage, immediately transfer the cookies to wire racks to cool completely.

Hot Buttered Rum Meltaways
(dusted with powdered sugar)
and Golden Fruitcake Nuggets

Golden Fruitcake Nuggets

Makes about 2 dozen (1½-inch) squares

Fruitcake fans and foes no longer have any reason to disagree. Chock-full of dried fruit, heavily spiced, and bound with little more than honey, these candy-like cookies are moist and delicious.

Complexity:

Active Time:

Type:

Bar

Prep Talk: Though not essential, a candy thermometer is helpful in Step 4. Store in airtight containers at room temperature for 5 to 7 days. Because of their high honey content, the cookies will be soft and chewy to start and will get softer over time. Never stack the cookies directly on top of one another, and always store under the driest possible conditions in airtight parchment paper–lined containers.

1 cup whole hazelnuts, toasted, skins rubbed off, and coarsely chopped
1 cup blanched slivered almonds, toasted and coarsely chopped
1 cup coarsely chopped candied orange peel
1 cup citron, finely chopped
2 tablespoons finely chopped crystallized ginger
1 teaspoon finely grated lemon zest
½ cup plus 2 tablespoons all-purpose flour
1¼ teaspoons ground cinnamon
½ teaspoon ground cardamom
³⁄₈ teaspoon ground coriander
³⁄₈ teaspoon ground cloves
½ teaspoon freshly grated nutmeg
Pinch ground white pepper
¾ cup granulated sugar
¾ cup honey
2 tablespoons unsalted butter, cut into tablespoon-size pieces

Powdered sugar (for dusting the cookie bottoms)

1. Line the bottom and sides of a 9-inch square baking pan with parchment paper. Fix the paper in place with a small amount of butter in each pan corner; then lightly coat the paper with nonstick cooking spray. Avoid excessive greasing of the pan, as this will make it more difficult to remove the bars later.

2. Position a rack in the center of the oven and preheat the oven to 300 degrees F.

3. Mix the nuts, orange peel, citron, crystallized ginger, lemon zest, flour, spices, and pepper together in a large bowl, taking care to break apart any candied fruit or ginger pieces that may be stuck together.

4. Place the sugar and honey in a medium (3-quart) saucepan. Stir until the sugar is evenly moistened; then add the butter pieces. Place the mixture over medium to medium-high heat and bring to a gentle boil. Reduce the heat to low and cook, stirring occasionally, until the syrup registers 246 to 248 degrees F on a candy thermometer. (Alternatively, the syrup will be ready when a small drop forms a firm but malleable ball when placed in ice water.) Immediately pour the hot syrup over the fruit-flour mixture and stir until well blended. Work quickly or the syrup will cool and stiffen, making the batter difficult to spread. Transfer the batter to the prepared pan and spread to a uniform thickness with a small offset spatula.

5. Bake 40 to 42 minutes, or until bubbly and lightly browned around the edges but still soft in the center. (The batter will harden considerably as it cools.) Transfer the pan to a wire rack and let the fruitcake cool completely in the pan.

6. Invert the pan onto a cutting board. If the fruitcake does not fall out on its own, loosen it by running a small knife along the edge of the pan and rapping the pan against your work surface. Peel the parchment paper off the fruitcake and invert the fruitcake again so the top is right side up. Using a sharp knife, trim the fruitcake block to a perfect square; then cut into 1½-inch squares.

7. To keep the bars from sticking to the bottom of the storage container, lightly dust the cookie bottoms with powdered sugar before storing.

Variation: Cocoa-Date Fruitcake Nuggets

(Pictured p. 131, center of box)

1. In Step 3 (p. 137), substitute 1 cup coarsely chopped pecan halves for the almonds and 1 teaspoon orange zest for the lemon zest. Omit the citron, crystallized ginger, and 2 tablespoons flour. Add ½ cup coarsely chopped dried tart cherries; ¾ cup chopped dried, pitted dates (stems removed); ¼ cup chopped dried black Mission figs (stems removed); and 2 tablespoons unsweetened non-alkalized cocoa powder. Mix well.

2. Proceed as directed in Steps 4 to 7 on page 137. *Note:* When done, this variation will not be as bubbly around the edges.

Hot Buttered Rum Meltaways

Makes about 3 dozen (1¾-inch) cookies

Laced with rum, nutmeg, cinnamon, and cloves, these downy soft cookies evoke one of the season's most famous libations. *Note:* Remember, never substitute pre-ground nutmeg for freshly grated, as the former can be harsh and bitter. For kids, omit the rum and rum extract.

Complexity:	Active Time:	Type:
1		Drop; hand-shaped

Prep Talk: Store in airtight containers at room temperature up to 1 week.

2¼ cups sifted cake flour
2½ teaspoons freshly grated nutmeg, plus extra for sprinkling
½ teaspoon ground cinnamon
⅜ teaspoon ground cloves
¼ teaspoon salt
1 cup (2 sticks) unsalted butter, slightly softened
1¼ cups sifted powdered sugar, divided; plus extra as needed for re-coating cookies
1 tablespoon dark rum
1½ teaspoons pure vanilla extract
1¼ teaspoons rum extract

1. Position a rack in the center of the oven and preheat the oven to 400 degrees F. Line two or more cookie sheets with parchment paper.

2. Stir the flour, spices, and salt together in a medium bowl. Set aside for use in Step 4.

3. Place the butter and ¾ cup powdered sugar in the bowl of an electric mixer fitted with a paddle attachment. Stir to bring the ingredients together (and to keep the sugar from scattering in the next step.)

4. Beat the butter and sugar on medium speed until light and fluffy, about 1 to 2 minutes. Slowly add the rum and extracts, and blend well. Turn the mixer to low speed and gradually add the dry ingredients. Mix just until combined.

5. Roll the dough between your palms into 1-inch balls and place about 2 inches apart on the prepared cookie sheets. For the most uniform balls, first portion the dough into 1-inch mounds using a level 1⅜-inch (#70) scoop or 2 level teaspoons per mound; then roll into perfect balls. (If the butter was too soft to start, the dough may be sticky and hard to handle. The cookies will also be more likely to flatten in the heat of the oven. Chill as needed until easily shaped.)

6. Bake 9 to 11 minutes, or until puffed, set, and lightly browned on the bottom. Using an offset spatula, immediately transfer the cookies to wire racks to cool. (If you pick up the cookies while they are hot, you can misshape them.) While the cookies are still warm, sift the remaining powdered sugar evenly over the tops. Cool completely before storing.

7. Right before serving, sift more powdered sugar over the cookies (as needed to re-coat them) and then sprinkle with grated nutmeg to taste.

Cranberry-Pistachio Biscotti
Makes 2 to 2½ dozen (1 x 4½-inch) biscotti

Basic Biscotti gets decked for the season with cranberries and pistachios—a festive and flavorful riff.

Complexity:	Active Time:	Type:
1		Hand-shaped

Prep Talk: Store in airtight containers at room temperature up to 1 week.

1 recipe Basic Biscotti (p. 142)
2¼ teaspoons pure pistachio (p. 156) or almond extract
½ cup shelled pistachios (preferably unsalted), skins rubbed off and coarsely chopped
½ cup dried cranberries, coarsely chopped

Decoration (optional)
About ⅓ cup shelled pistachios (preferably unsalted), skins rubbed off and finely chopped

1. Prepare 1 recipe Basic Biscotti as instructed on page 142, except add the pistachio (or almond) extract along with the vanilla extract in Step 3. Stir in the pistachios and cranberries at the end of Step 4 before shaping into loaves as directed in Step 5.

2. Decorate (optional). Gently press the remaining pistachios into the tops of the loaves before transferring them to parchment paper–lined cookie sheets.

3. Bake and cool as directed on page 142. (Remember, do not overbake the loaves or let them cool for more than a few minutes, or they will be difficult to cut without cracking.)

Chocolate–Peanut Butter Yule Logs

Makes 8 to 8½ dozen (¾ x 2¼- to 2½-inch) logs

Your guests will definitely get fired up about these cookies. Two flavors of the same dough—one peanut butter and another cocoa-peanut butter—are rolled together and then spritzed into festive logs.

Complexity:

1

Active Time:

Type:

Pressed (or piped)

Prep Talk: Store in airtight containers at room temperature up to 2 weeks. *Note:* The dipping chocolate will look its best if applied just before serving. It can turn dull and streaky if stored at temperatures in excess of 65 to 70 degrees F or under humid conditions. However, avoid refrigeration (except to set the chocolate), as it will soften the cookies.

1¼ cups all-purpose flour
¾ teaspoon baking soda
½ teaspoon baking powder
¼ teaspoon salt
½ cup (½ stick) butter-flavored shortening
½ cup creamy peanut butter
½ cup granulated sugar
½ cup firmly packed light brown sugar
1 large egg
1 teaspoon pure vanilla extract
1 tablespoon unsweetened non-alkalized cocoa powder
1 tablespoon powdered sugar

Decoration (optional)
8 ounces premium milk chocolate, melted
1 cup honey-roasted peanuts, finely chopped

1. Position a rack in the center of the oven and preheat the oven to 375 degrees F. Line two or more cookie sheets with parchment paper.

2. Stir the flour, baking soda, baking powder, and salt together in a small bowl. Set aside for use in Step 4.

3. Place the shortening and peanut butter in the bowl of an electric mixer fitted with a paddle attachment. Beat on medium speed until blended. Gradually add the sugars and continue to beat until the mixture is light, fluffy, and free of any brown sugar lumps, about 1 to 2 minutes. Scrape down the sides of the bowl as needed to ensure even mixing.

4. Add the egg and vanilla extract, and mix until well combined. Turn the mixer to low speed and gradually add the dry ingredients, mixing just until incorporated.

5. Divide the dough evenly into two portions. To one half, add the cocoa powder and powdered sugar. Mix or knead until the dough is a uniform light brown color. Leave the other half as-is.

6. Divide the plain peanut butter dough into two parts and do the same with the cocoa-flavored dough. Roll each portion into a 1-inch-diameter log, about 10 to 11 inches long. (No flouring of your work surface is necessary.) Place a cocoa and a peanut butter log side by side on your work surface. Place the remaining peanut butter log on top of the cocoa log, and the remaining cocoa log on top of the peanut butter log. Roll all four logs together to form one big log, about 1¾ inches in diameter and 15 to 16 inches long. Cut the log into 4 (3½- to 4-inch) lengths.

7. Insert one length into a cookie press and fit the end of the press with a ⅜-inch star-shaped pastry tip. If the tip is too big to fit on the outside of the press coupler (tip attachment), insert it inside the coupler so it sits within the press chamber. (Piping through a traditional pastry bag is possible, but because the dough is firm, this approach will require a lot of force. To avoid hand fatigue, a cookie press is a far better option.) Wrap the other logs with plastic so they don't dry out while you work with the first.

8. Hold the cookie press at a 45-degree angle to the cookie sheet and press the dough into small logs, each about ½ inch in diameter and 2¼ inches long. Space the logs about 1 inch apart. (The logs will crack along their edges, creating a rough-hewn effect.) Replenish the cookie press with additional lengths of dough as needed.

9. Bake 5 to 7 minutes, or until set and tinged a slightly darker shade of brown on top. Cool on the pan just until firm enough to transfer to wire racks without breaking. Cool completely before decorating or storing.

10. Decorate (optional). Dip both ends of each cookie in melted chocolate and then sprinkle with the peanuts. Place the dipped cookies on a parchment paper-lined cookie sheet and transfer to the refrigerator for a few minutes, just until the chocolate is completely set.

COOKIE-CUTTER APPROACHES

This chapter includes nine simple and infinitely adaptable cookie and icing recipes—the very classics that appear time and time again in my cookie swaps and in different variations throughout this book.

Basic Biscotti

Makes 2 to 2½ dozen (1 x 4½-inch) biscotti

When I am need of a distinctive cookie, biscotti are a great pick. Tall and crunchy, they are a welcome contrast to soft and stout bar and drop cookies.

Complexity:

Active Time:

Type:

Hand-shaped

Prep Talk: Store in airtight containers at room temperature up to 1 week.

2¼ cups all-purpose flour

1½ teaspoons baking powder

½ teaspoon salt

½ cup (1 stick) unsalted butter, softened

1 cup granulated sugar

2 large eggs

1 teaspoon pure vanilla extract (increase to 2 teaspoons if you do not add other flavorings)

Additional flavorings, if desired

½ to 1 cup nuts of choice, chopped

1. Position a rack in the center of the oven and preheat the oven to 325 degrees F. Line two cookie sheets with parchment paper.

2. Stir the flour, baking powder, and salt together in a small bowl. Set aside for use in Step 4.

3. Using an electric mixer (see "Stand-in" below) fitted with a paddle attachment, cream the butter until smooth. Gradually add the sugar and beat on medium to medium-high speed until well blended, about 1 minute. Add the eggs one at a time, beating well after each addition. Scrape down the sides of the bowl as needed to ensure even mixing. Add the vanilla extract and any additional flavorings, and mix well.

4. Turn the mixer to low speed and gradually add the dry ingredients, blending just until incorporated. Stir in the nuts.

5. On a lightly floured surface, shape the dough into 2 (3 x 8-inch) rectangular loaves, each about ¾ inch thick. Place the loaves 4 to 5 inches apart on one cookie sheet and bake until slightly golden around the edges, about 30 minutes. Do not overbake, or the dough may crack upon cutting in the next step.

6. Slide the loaves, one at a time, onto a cutting board and immediately slice into ½-inch-thick cross sections. (Do not cool for more than a few minutes, as the dough will be more likely to crack.) Re-line the cookie sheet with parchment paper.

7. Lay the slices cut side down on the two cookie sheets and return the first sheet to the oven. Bake 13 to 15 minutes, flipping the cookies once or twice during baking to promote even browning. When done, the biscotti should be light brown and quite firm. Immediately transfer to wire racks and cool completely before storing. (The biscotti will become even crisper upon cooling.) Repeat with the remaining sheet of biscotti.

Stand-in

• While I personally rely on the horsepower of an electric stand mixer for most cookie recipes, every recipe in this book can be prepared with a hand-held electric mixer or by hand. You may have to work harder or longer, but the results will still be tasty.

Shortbread, Straight Up

Makes about 2 ½ dozen (2 ¼- to 2 ½-inch) cookies

A buttery blank canvas, shortbread shows off any flavor to the fullest. Substitute other nuts for the almonds, or mix in herbs, citrus zest, or chopped dried fruit—whatever suits your party theme best.

Complexity:

Active Time:

Type:

Rolled

Prep Talk: The dough must be chilled 1 to 2 hours before rolling and cutting. The dough can be frozen up to 1 month with minimal loss of flavor if wrapped tightly in plastic and then foil. Store baked cookies in airtight containers at room temperature no longer than 2 weeks.

2 cups all-purpose flour, divided
½ cup blanched slivered almonds
½ teaspoon salt
1 cup (2 sticks) unsalted butter, softened
¼ cup granulated sugar
¼ cup sifted powdered sugar
1 teaspoon pure vanilla extract

About 2 tablespoons granulated sugar (for sprinkling)

1. In a food processor fitted with a metal blade, process 2 tablespoons flour and the almonds until the nuts are finely ground but not pasty. Add the remaining flour and salt, and process until well combined. Set aside for use in Step 2.

2. Place the butter and sugars in the bowl of an electric mixer fitted with a paddle attachment. Stir to bring the ingredients together; then beat on medium to medium-high speed until light and fluffy, about 1 minute. Turn the mixer to low speed and add the vanilla extract. Gradually add the flour mixture, blending just until incorporated. Scrape down the sides of the bowl as needed to ensure even mixing.

3. Flatten the dough into a disk and wrap tightly in plastic. Refrigerate 1 to 2 hours, or until firm enough to roll without sticking.

4. Place a rack in the center of the oven and preheat the oven to 300 degrees F. Line two or more cookie sheets with parchment paper.

FAQ: **Why, when, and how should nuts and seeds be toasted?**
Toasting nuts and seeds brings their essential oils to the surface and enhances their flavor. For relatively long-baking recipes, such as Basic Biscotti (opposite), there's no need to toast these items in advance since they'll toast in the course of cookie baking. However, for short-baking cookies and bars where the nuts or seeds are buried in the interior, these goodies are best toasted before they go into the batter. To toast, simply spread the nuts (preferably whole) or seeds in a single layer on a cookie sheet and set in a preheated 375 degree F oven. Bake until fragrant and lightly browned, watching closely and tossing occasionally to avoid burning. Small seeds will toast in a matter of a few minutes.

5. Roll the dough on a lightly floured surface to a ¼-inch thickness. Cut with a 2 ¼- to 2 ½-inch round, oval, or other cookie cutter. Using an offset spatula (see "FAQ" on p. 146), carefully transfer the cookies to the prepared cookie sheets, spacing them about 1 inch apart.

6. Sprinkle the remaining sugar evenly over the cookie tops to thinly coat them. Bake 25 to 30 minutes, or until lightly browned on the bottom and firm to the touch. Immediately transfer to wire racks with an offset spatula to prevent breakage. Cool completely before storing.

Brown Sugar–Pecan Sweethearts (p. 25), a Shortbread, Straight Up variation

Classic Icebox Cookie Dough

Makes 1½ to 2 dozen (2 ½- to 3-inch) cookies

Tinted two ways, this basic butter dough can be shaped into a plethora of dazzling patterns. See the shaping methods (opposite) for four of my favorite styles, or feel free to get creative.

Complexity:

(varies with shaping method)

Active Time:

Type:
Hand-shaped; rolled; icebox

Prep Talk: For best results, the dough must be chilled for 1 to 2 hours before shaping and then for another 1 to 2 hours before slicing—so plan accordingly. Shaped dough can be frozen up to 1 month with minimal loss of flavor if tightly wrapped in plastic and then foil. When you're ready for cookies, simply slice and bake. Store baked cookies in airtight containers up to 5 days. For the crunchiest eating, enjoy within 24 hours.

2 ½ cups all-purpose flour
½ teaspoon baking soda
¼ teaspoon salt
1 cup (2 sticks) unsalted butter, softened
1¼ cups sifted powdered sugar
¼ cup plus 2 tablespoons granulated sugar
1 large egg
¾ teaspoon pure vanilla extract (increase to 1½ teaspoons if you do not add other flavorings)
Additional flavorings, if desired
Soft gel food coloring of your choice, to desired shade (p. 152)

Egg Wash
1 large egg white, lightly beaten with 2 teaspoons water

1. Stir the flour, baking soda, and salt together in a small bowl. Set aside for use in Step 3.

2. Place the butter and sugars in the bowl of an electric mixer. Stir to bring the ingredients together (and to prevent the sugar from scattering in the next step).

3. Fit the mixer with a paddle attachment and beat the butter mixture on medium-low speed until light and creamy, about 1 minute. Add the egg, vanilla extract, and any additional flavorings, and beat until smooth, scraping down the sides of the bowl as needed. Gradually add the flour mixture and mix just until incorporated.

4. Divide the dough in half and add the food coloring to the first half of the dough. Stir until the color is evenly distributed. Leave the other half of the dough as-is.

5. Flatten each portion of dough into a disk, wrap in plastic, and refrigerate 1 to 2 hours. (Chilling time varies with shaping method; see "Icebox Cookie Shaping Methods," opposite, for details.)

6. On a lightly floured surface, shape the dough into logs in one of four ways. (Again, see "Icebox Cookie Shaping Methods.") Wrap the finished log(s) tightly in plastic to hold their shape and freeze 1 to 2 hours before slicing. The dough should be quite firm yet not so hard it can't be easily sliced. (Stand round logs on end to avoid flattening on one side.)

7. Position a rack in the center of the oven and preheat the oven to 375 degrees F. Line two or more cookie sheets with parchment paper.

8. Work with one chilled log at a time, leaving any others in the freezer until you're ready to slice them. Cut the log crosswise into 3/16- to ¼-inch-thick slices. Arrange the slices 1½ to 2 inches apart on the prepared cookie sheets and trim the edges, if desired, using a cookie cutter of your choice. (A round cutter works well for Beach Ball, Halvesie, and Pinwheel, whereas a square or star-shaped one works well for Pinstripe.)

9. Bake 7 to 10 minutes, or until lightly browned on the bottom. The tops should show minimal discoloration. (Thick slices or cookies wider than about 3 inches will bake closer to 10 minutes.)

10. Immediately transfer the cookies to wire racks and cool completely before storing. *Note:* If the cookies aren't sliced to a uniform thickness before baking, they can spread unevenly. When this occurs, I often trim the edges with a cookie cutter after baking, while the cookies are still hot.

Pictured from upper left to lower right: Beach Ball, Pinwheel, Pinstripe, and Halvesie.

Icebox Cookie Shaping Methods

Note: Shape the dough only after it has been chilled. For easiest handling, chill the dough 1 to 2 hours when shaping the dough directly into logs (i.e., for Beach Ball and Halvesie) and closer to 2 hours when instructions call for rolling the dough into thin rectangles or squares before shaping it into logs (i.e., for Pinwheel and Pinstripe). If the dough gets too soft, return it to the refrigerator or freezer until it can be handled without sticking. Remember to wrap and freeze the finished log(s) as instructed in Step 6 (opposite) before slicing.

Beach Ball: Shape the white portion of the dough into a 2¼-inch-diameter log, about 4 to 5 inches long. Repeat with the tinted dough, trying to match the dimensions of the white log as closely as possible. Wrap the logs tightly in plastic wrap and freeze until quite firm. Unwrap and cut each log lengthwise into six equal wedges. Replace every other wedge in the tinted

log with a wedge from the white log, and vice versa, affixing the wedges to one another with a small amount of egg wash (opposite). Press each log together to make sure the wedges are firmly in place.

Pinwheel: Roll the white dough into a 9 x 15-inch rectangle, about ⅛ inch thick. Repeat with the tinted dough. Lightly brush the white rectangle with egg wash and carefully slide the tinted rectangle on top. Gently press the two layers together. Trim the dough into a perfect 8 x 14-inch rectangle. Starting at one of the smaller sides, roll the dough into a 2¼-inch-diameter log, about 8 inches long. As you roll, brush off any excess flour on the back of the white dough so that the dough clings to itself. Fix the free end in place with egg wash as needed.

Pinstripe: Roll the white dough into an 11 x 11-inch square, about ⅛ to ³⁄₁₆ inch thick. Repeat with the tinted dough. Lightly brush the white square with egg wash and carefully slide the tinted square directly on top. Trim to a perfect 10 x 10-inch square. Cut the square into eight small rectangles, each 2½ x 5 inches. Stack one rectangle on top of the other, alternating the white and tinted layers. Affix the rectangles to one another with egg wash and gently press together. (You should have a stack about 2½ inches tall and 2½ x 5 inches at the base.)

Halvesie: Shape the white portion of the dough into a 2¼-inch-diameter log, about 4 to 5 inches long. Repeat with the tinted dough, trying to match the dimensions of the white log as closely as possible. Wrap the logs in plastic wrap and freeze until quite firm. Unwrap and cut each log in half lengthwise. Affix one white half to a tinted half with a small amount of egg wash and gently press together. Repeat with the remaining white and tinted halves to make a second log.

Cutout Cookie Gingerbread

Makes about 6 dozen (2 ¾-inch) cookies

This dough is crisp and delicate—perfect for small decorated cutouts and even lightweight gingerbread construction, such as the potted roses in "Not Your Garden-Variety Garden Party" (p. 49).

Complexity:	Active Time:	Type:
		Rolled

Prep Talk: The dough must be chilled about 3 hours before rolling and cutting. The dough can be frozen up to 1 month with minimal loss of flavor if wrapped tightly in plastic and then foil. Store baked cookies in airtight containers at room temperature no longer than 1 to 2 weeks; for maximum flavor, enjoy within 3 to 5 days.

5 cups all-purpose flour
2 ½ teaspoons ground ginger
1 ¼ teaspoons ground cinnamon
1 teaspoon ground cloves
1 ½ teaspoons baking soda
½ teaspoon salt
1 cup (1 stick) shortening
1 cup granulated sugar
1 large egg
1 cup mild molasses
2 tablespoons white vinegar

1. Stir the flour, spices, baking soda, and salt together in a large bowl. Set aside for use in Step 4.

2. Using an electric mixer fitted with a paddle attachment, beat the shortening and sugar until well combined. Add the egg and beat on medium-high speed until light and fluffy, about 1 to 2 minutes. Scrape down the sides of the bowl as needed to ensure even mixing.

3. Turn the mixer to medium speed and add the molasses and vinegar. Mix well. Scrape down the sides of the bowl as needed.

4. Remove the bowl from the mixer and stir in the dry ingredients by hand, mixing just to combine. (Make sure the dry ingredients are fully incorporated, however. There should be no dry spots.)

5. Divide the dough into two equal portions and flatten each portion into a disk. Wrap each disk tightly in plastic and refrigerate about 3 hours, or until firm enough to roll without sticking.

6. Position a rack in the center of the oven and preheat the oven to 375 degrees F. Line two or more cookie sheets with parchment paper.

7. Work with one disk of dough at a time. Roll the dough on a lightly floured surface to a ⅛-inch thickness. Cut out assorted shapes using your favorite cookie cutters. Carefully transfer the cookies to the prepared cookie sheets with an offset spatula (see "FAQ" below), leaving about 1 inch between each cutout.

8. For 2 ½-inch cookies, bake 8 to 10 minutes, or until firm and tinged slightly darker brown around the edges. (Baking time varies tremendously with cookie size and thickness.) Let particularly long or delicately shaped cookies cool 1 to 2 minutes on the cookie sheet before transferring to wire racks. Otherwise, immediately transfer the cookies. Cool completely before frosting with Royal Icing or storing.

FAQ: **How is an offset spatula different than a regular one?**
An offset spatula has a blade that is offset at a 45-degree angle relative to the handle. A small offset spatula (with a blade about ¾ x 3¼ inches) is the ideal tool for leveling batter and spreading icings, especially when you need to reach deep into a baking pan. A wider offset spatula (with a blade at least 2½ inches across) is handy for transferring warm cookies to racks or unbaked cutout cookies to cookie sheets. The offset makes it easier to get the blade underneath cookies, and the wide blade gives soft cookies more support than the typical straight, thin-bladed spatula.

Construction Gingerbread

Makes about 6 dozen (2 ¾-inch) cookies, or the equivalent of 3 (5 x 5 x 5-inch) gingerbread boxes (pictured, p. 130)

Here bread flour is substituted for all-purpose flour to make a gingerbread dough that is sturdier and less prone to spreading than standard cutout cookie dough. This protein-rich recipe is an ideal building block for 3-D and large 2-D construction projects intended primarily for display, such as the gingerbread boxes (p. 130) and wreath (p. 129) in "Deck the Halls."

Complexity:	Active Time:	Type:
		Rolled

Prep Talk: Though not essential, a candy thermometer is helpful in Step 2. Chill the dough several hours or until it is easily rolled without sticking. Due to its high bread flour content, the dough is naturally quite stiff. If you find it too difficult to roll straight from the fridge, let it soften at room temperature about ½ hour. The dough can be frozen up to 1 month with minimal loss of flavor if wrapped tightly in plastic and then foil. Once baked, cookies will stay crisp and construction-ready for several months in airtight containers, stored at room temperature. Flavor will dissipate over time, so if you intend to eat your construction project, bake the cookie pieces no more than 1 week ahead.

5 cups bread flour
2 tablespoons ground cinnamon
1 tablespoon ground cloves
1 tablespoon ground ginger
1¼ teaspoons baking soda
¼ teaspoon salt
1 cup plus 2 tablespoons granulated sugar
½ cup (1 stick) plus 7 tablespoons margarine, cut into tablespoon-
    size pieces
¾ cup corn syrup
¼ cup plus 2 tablespoons whole milk

1. Stir the flour, spices, baking soda, and salt together in a large bowl. Set aside for use in Step 3.

2. Combine the sugar, margarine, corn syrup, and milk in a large (6½-quart) nonreactive (stainless steel or coated) saucepan. Place the pan over medium to medium-high heat. Cook, stirring frequently, until the butter has completely melted and the mixture is the consistency of thick syrup. (The syrup should look cloudy, with minimal oil separation from the margarine, and feel slightly warm to the touch. When ready, it will register 115 to 125 degrees F on a candy thermometer.)

3. Remove the pan from the heat and add half of the dry ingredients. Mix until lump-free. Add the remaining dry ingredients and mix until the flour is just incorporated. The dough will be shiny and somewhat sticky at this point, but do not add more flour. (Excess flour and handling will only toughen the dough.) Cover the surface of the dough lightly with plastic wrap and cool to room temperature. (If left uncovered, the dough can dry out.)

4. Divide the dough into two equal portions and flatten each portion into a disk. Wrap each disk tightly in plastic and refrigerate several hours, or until firm enough to roll without sticking.

5. Position a rack in the center of the oven and preheat the oven to 375 degrees F. Line two or more cookie sheets with parchment paper.

6. Work with one disk of dough at a time. For large 3-D construction projects (bigger than about 5 x 5 x 5 inches, the size of the boxes in "Deck the Halls"), roll the dough on a lightly floured surface to a ³⁄₁₆- to ¼-inch thickness. For smaller projects, roll the dough thinner, but no less than ⅛ inch thick. Cut out assorted shapes using your favorite cookie cutters. Alternatively, cut out cardboard templates for your project pieces, set them atop the rolled gingerbread, and cut around them with a sharp paring knife. Using an offset spatula, carefully transfer your cookie cutouts to the prepared cookie sheets, leaving about 1 inch between each piece. If your pieces are very large or difficult to handle with a spatula, cut them directly on the cookie sheet. *Note:* Place cookies of similar size on the same cookie sheet to ensure that all cookies bake at roughly the same rate.

7. Bake 10 to 12 minutes for small (2½- to 3-inch) cookies and closer to 15 minutes for large (5- to 6-inch) cookies. Baking time varies tremendously with cookie size and thickness. When done, the cookies should be firm to the touch and well browned. For large-scale support pieces, it is especially important to bake the cookies all the way through. While the cookies are still warm from the oven, trim any uneven or misshapen edges, if desired.

8. Cool 1 to 2 minutes on the cookie sheet before transferring to wire racks. Cool completely before assembling with thick Royal Icing or storing. (The cookies will harden considerably as they cool.)

How to Make Gingerbread Boxes and Baskets

. . . such as those pictured right and on pages 32 and 130:

- Start by creating templates for the pieces that will compose the sides and bottom of your project. Draw the desired shapes onto 3-ply cardboard and cut them out. Double-check to make sure your templates fit together as you envisioned. Adjust any templates as needed.

- Mix, cut, and bake the gingerbread pieces as described in Construction Gingerbread (pp. 146 and 147), using your templates as cutting guides.

- Before decorating or assembling any pieces, check to be sure they fit snugly together in 3-D. If they do not, straighten any bumpy or misshapen edges by gently shaving them with a paring knife.

- Box and basket sides can look beautiful undecorated, but feel free to top-coat them with Royal Icing (p. 151) or to further embellish them with wafer papers (p. 154) or other decorative techniques. (For the May Day baskets, pictured right, I first top-coated the sides and then applied wafer paper, preprinted in a toile pattern.) Dry all decorations thoroughly before proceeding to the next step.

- Spread Royal Icing, thinned to top-coating consistency (p. 152), on the back of each piece. The added icing reinforces and seals the cookies so they stay straight and firm even in the face of humidity.

- Once the icing has dried, fill a parchment pastry cone (p. 153) with thick Royal Icing and glue the pieces together at the seams. If the pieces slip or have difficulty standing up on their own, thicken the icing with powdered sugar. (The icing can almost never be too thick for this step.) Use wadded paper towels or other lightweight objects, if needed, to prop the pieces in place. Pre-made fondant pieces, such as the bows and handles on the baskets in "Spring Fling," can also be glued on in this step. (See "Fun with Fondant," page 155, for bow- and handle-making tips.)

- Let the "glue" dry thoroughly, ideally overnight, before moving your creation. If stored in airtight containers, 3-D gingerbread projects will remain presentation-ready for many months.

Gingerbread May Day Baskets

Signature Sugar Cookie Dough
Makes about 2 dozen (2 ¾-inch) cookies

The foundation of the many signature sugar cookies in the swaps, this recipe is chameleon-like in its ability to assume different flavors. Match its taste to the season by adding zippy citrus zest in spring and summer and pungent spices and extracts in winter and fall.

Complexity:	Active Time:	Type:
		Rolled

Prep Talk: For easiest handling, the dough must be chilled at least 3 hours before rolling and cutting. The dough can be frozen up to 1 month with minimal loss of flavor if wrapped tightly in plastic and then foil. Store baked cookies in airtight containers at room temperature up to 1 week. (Cookies frosted with Royal Icing should also be stored at room temperature, as refrigeration can cause the icing colors to bleed and the cookies to soften.)

2 cups all-purpose flour
1½ teaspoons baking powder
¼ teaspoon salt
6 tablespoons (¾ stick) unsalted butter, softened
⅓ cup (⅓ stick) shortening
¾ cup granulated sugar
1 large egg
1 tablespoon whole milk
1 teaspoon pure vanilla extract
Additional flavorings, if desired (see "FAQ," right)

1. Combine the flour, baking powder, and salt in a small bowl. Set aside for use in Step 4.

2. Using an electric mixer fitted with a paddle attachment, beat the butter and shortening on medium speed until creamy. Gradually add the sugar and beat until light and fluffy, about 1 to 2 minutes.

3. Whisk the egg, milk, vanilla extract, and any additional flavorings (see "Variations," this page) together in another bowl. Slowly add the liquid to the butter mixture and blend thoroughly on low to medium speed until the mixture is smooth. Scrape down the sides of the bowl as needed to ensure even mixing.

4. Turn the mixer to low speed and gradually add the flour mixture, mixing just until incorporated.

5. Flatten the dough into a disk, wrap tightly in plastic, and refrigerate at least 3 hours, or until firm enough to roll without sticking.

6. Position a rack in the center of the oven and preheat the oven to 375 degrees F. Line two cookie sheets with parchment paper.

7. Roll the dough on a lightly floured surface to a ⅛-inch thickness. Cut out assorted shapes with your favorite cookie cutters. Carefully transfer the cookies to the prepared cookie sheets with an offset spatula, leaving about 1 inch between each cutout.

8. Bake 8 to 10 minutes, or until lightly browned around the edges. (Baking time varies with cookie size and thickness.) Let particularly long or delicately shaped cookies cool 1 to 2 minutes on the cookie sheet before transferring to wire racks. Otherwise, immediately transfer to racks and cool completely before frosting with Royal Icing or storing.

Variations:

Lemon-Lime: Reduce the vanilla extract to ½ teaspoon and add 2 teaspoons finely grated lemon zest and 1 teaspoon pure lime oil.

Cinnamon: Add 1½ teaspoons ground cinnamon to the dry ingredients and reduce the vanilla extract to ¾ teaspoon. *Note:* The ground cinnamon will tint the dough pale brown.

Anise: Reduce the vanilla extract to ½ teaspoon and add ½ teaspoon anise extract. Sprinkle each cookie sheet with 1½ teaspoons whole anise seed before placing and baking the cookies.

FAQ: **Are certain flavorings preferred for cookies and icings?**
Opt for 100 percent natural extracts and oils whenever possible. The reason: These flavorings taste better. Though oils and extracts of the same flavor may be interchanged, oils tend to be more potent and will also hold up better in the oven. When substituting oil for extract, I generally start with about one quarter of the specified quantity of extract and gradually add more oil to taste. For sources, see page 156.

Ganache
Makes about 2½ cups
This decadent chocolate and cream blend easily morphs from satiny glaze to creamy filling simply by setting it in the fridge. It can also be made with either dark or white chocolate with only minor adjustments.

Complexity:	Active Time:	Type:
1		N/A

12 ounces premium semisweet chocolate (see "FAQ," right), finely chopped or ground in a food processor

1½ cups heavy cream

1 tablespoon light corn syrup

1. Place the chopped (or ground) chocolate in a large bowl so it forms a shallow layer. Set aside.

2. Pour the cream into a medium (3-quart) nonreactive (stainless steel or coated) saucepan. Place over medium to medium-high heat and scald the cream. (That is, heat the cream to just below the boiling point. The cream will put off steam, but no bubbles should break on its surface.)

3. Immediately strain the hot cream through a fine-meshed sieve directly onto the chocolate. Let the mixture sit 1 to 2 minutes without stirring, and then gently whisk until the chocolate is entirely melted. (If the chocolate does not completely melt, set the bowl over barely simmering water in a double boiler and stir regularly until smooth. Do not overheat, or the ganache may break.) Stir in the corn syrup.

4. To use the ganache as a glaze, pour it while lukewarm. Alternatively, for piping ganache, pour it into a shallow pan to a ½- to ¾-inch depth, cover, and refrigerate 20 to 25 minutes, or until slightly thickened. Stir occasionally during chilling to maintain a uniform consistency. (Hard, overchilled pieces of ganache should be broken up, as they can easily clog pastry tips when piping.) Chilling time will vary with starting ganache temperature, refrigerator temperature, and depth of the ganache. Watch the ganache closely, as it can quickly overchill and become difficult to pipe.

Variation: White Chocolate

Makes about 1¾ cups

Substitute premium white chocolate (see "FAQ" on this page) for the semisweet chocolate in Step 1. Reduce the cream to ¾ cup and proceed as directed above.

Italian Buttercream

Makes about 4½ cups

Unlike classic American buttercream, which consists primarily of butter and powdered sugar, this icing starts with whipped egg whites and ends up fluffy and light—ideal for cookie toppings and fillings.

Notes: 1) Though the egg whites in this recipe are heated, pasteurized whites can be substituted to minimize the risk of food-borne illness associated with raw eggs. Use about 2 tablespoons pasteurized whites for every large white. 2) If a recipe calls for any fraction of Italian Buttercream, it is best to make a full batch and portion off what you need. (The ingredient quantities below are too small to mix practically in any smaller quantity.) Leftover icing may be frozen as described below for later use.

Complexity:	Active Time:	Type:
2		N/A

4 large egg whites, room temperature (or 8 to 9 tablespoons pasteurized egg whites)

¼ teaspoon cream of tartar

⅔ cup granulated sugar

⅓ cup plus 1 tablespoon light corn syrup

1⅔ cups (3 sticks plus 2⅔ tablespoons) unsalted butter, softened

1 teaspoon pure vanilla extract (increase to 1 tablespoon if you do not add other flavorings)

Additional flavorings, if desired

1. Combine the egg whites and cream of tartar in the bowl of an

electric mixer fitted with a whip attachment. (*Note:* The bowl, whip attachment, and all mixing utensils should be completely free of fat, or the egg whites will not stiffen.) Beat on medium speed to firm peaks.

2. Meanwhile, combine the sugar and corn syrup in a large non-stick skillet, and stir to evenly moisten the sugar. Place the mixture over medium-high heat and bring to a boil, stirring as needed to make sure the sugar completely dissolves. Continue to boil approximately 30 seconds, until thick, syrupy, and bubbly through to the center.

3. Turn the mixer to medium-high speed and gradually add the hot sugar syrup in a slow, steady stream. (Do not stop the mixer while adding the syrup, or the egg whites can curdle.) Once all of the syrup has been incorporated, quickly scrape down the sides of the bowl, taking care not to scrape any hard crystallized sugar into the meringue. Resume beating at high speed until the meringue has cooled, about 7 to 10 minutes.

4. Add the butter 2 tablespoons at time, beating well after each addition. *Note:* The icing will initially deflate and look grainy but will get quite thick and glossy as more butter is incorporated.

5. Add the vanilla extract and additional flavorings, if desired, and mix well.

Royal Icing
Makes about 4 ½ cups, enough to top-coat
4 to 5 dozen (3-inch) cookies

This icing is by far my favorite frosting for cutout cookies. Because it contains high-protein egg whites, it dries quickly with minimal spreading; it also holds food coloring quite well with limited to no bleeding. Use this thick formulation as edible "glue" for gingerbread construction projects (p. 148), or adjust its consistency for other cookie decorating techniques. (See sidebar, this page, for consistency adjustments, and page 152 for decorating techniques.)

    Note: Since the egg whites in this recipe are not heated, it is best to use pasteurized whites to minimize the risk of food-borne illness, especially when serving the very young or old or those with compromised immune systems.

Complexity:	Active Time:	Type:
1		N/A

Prep Talk: Tinted icing is best used the day it is mixed because the color will dry more uniformly. Otherwise, the icing can be made 1 to 2 days ahead and stored in the fridge. Bring the icing to room temperature when ready to use and stir vigorously to restore its original consistency. Once applied to cookies, the icing should remain at room temperature so it sets into a crunchy candy-like coating. Important: Unless you're using the icing, always cover the surface flush with plastic wrap to prevent a crust from forming.

2 pounds powdered sugar
½ teaspoon cream of tartar
About 11 tablespoons pasteurized whites (or 5 large egg whites)
Flavoring, to taste
Soft gel food coloring (see "FAQ," p. 152) of your choice,
    to desired shade (optional)

1. Mix the powdered sugar and cream of tartar together in the bowl of an electric mixer. Stir in the egg whites by hand to moisten the sugar. Fit the electric mixer with a whip attachment and beat the mixture on low speed to evenly distribute the egg whites. Turn the mixer to medium-high speed and continue to beat about 2 minutes, until the icing is silky and very white. (The icing will lighten and thicken as you beat it.)

2. Beat in flavoring and/or food coloring, if desired. Mix well before using.

Consistency Adjustments for Royal Icing

The following consistency adjustments are approximate guidelines for a single batch of un-tinted Royal Icing. The addition of food coloring or flavoring, beating time, and normal variations in egg size can all affect the end consistency. If you make an adjustment and still think your icing is too thin or too thick for your application, simply adjust by adding powdered sugar to thicken or water to thin.

- **For outlining:** Add 1 to 2 tablespoons water. For crisp, well-defined outlines, start with 1 tablespoon water. If the icing is too thick to easily pipe through a small (⅛-inch) hole in a parchment pastry cone, gradually add more water. When piped, the icing should hold a thin line with no—or minimal—spreading.

- **For top-coating:** To avoid icing runoff on cookies under 2 inches, start by adding 2 to 3 tablespoons water. Gradually increase to 3 to 5 tablespoons as needed to improve spreadability on larger cookies.

- **For stenciling:** Add 3 to 4 tablespoons water, but remember, the exact quantity will vary with egg size and the other factors noted on page 151. The icing must be thin enough to easily spread into the stencil openings without leaving peaks or "tracks" when the spatula is lifted. At the same time, it must be sufficiently thick to keep from creeping under the stencil into areas where it is not wanted.

- **For beadwork:** About 4 tablespoons additional water works best, though exact quantities will vary, as noted above. At the proper consistency, a smooth, well-rounded dot should form when the icing is piped through a small (⅛-inch) opening in a parchment pastry cone. If the icing forms a peak, it is too thick. Conversely, if it spreads a great deal, it is too loose.

FAQ: Is a particular type of food coloring best for tinting Royal Icing?

While liquid, gel, paste, and soft gel food colorings can all be used to tint Royal Icing, I recommend soft gel coloring, a relatively thick, concentrated dye that comes in a container fitted with a dropper. A little soft gel coloring goes a very long way. The dropper also takes the guesswork out of getting the right color. (Just count the drops the first time you mix.) Chefmaster Liqua-Gel is a widely available brand of soft gel coloring, but for other brands and sources, see page 156.

Stand-ins

The next best choices are gel and paste food colorings. Both are very concentrated, but they come in small lidded jars and must be doled out with a toothpick or skewer—an often messy and unpredictable endeavor.

THE SUGAR ON TOP

Here you'll find a quick overview of the eleven cutout cookie decorating techniques introduced throughout the book, many of which use Royal Icing.

1. **Top-coating** (pictured, p. 42, bonnet tops) is the spreading of Royal Icing to create a smooth, glass-like coating over a broad area of the cookie. Thin the icing to top-coating consistency (this page) and use the handle-end of a small craft paintbrush or spoon to evenly distribute the icing over the cookie top. (The bristle-end may seem more logical, but since bristles spread and move, icing placement can be hard to control this way.) To avoid divots and rough spots, work quickly before the icing sets.

2. **Marbling** (pictured, p. 18) looks best when three or more Royal Icing colors are used—one for the top coat and two or more that get applied to the top coat with a parchment pastry cone (p. 153). Begin by mixing all icing colors to top-coating consistency (this page). Transfer all icings but the one for the top coat into separate parchment pastry cones, and cut a small tip in the hole of each cone. Apply a top coat with the remaining icing and then quickly pipe lines or dots of the other icing colors on top. Immediately draw a cake tester or toothpick through all of the icings to create a marbled effect. To avoid "tracks" in the icing, work quickly before any of the icings start to set. Countless patterns can be made by varying the way in which you pipe the icings onto the top coat and/or draw the cake tester through the icing. My best advice on creating patterns is to play—you will not be disappointed with the results!

3. **Outlining** (pictured, p. 97 and 111). To draw a cookie border, stripes, zigzags, or any other form of line, first fill a parchment pastry cone with Royal Icing thinned to outlining consistency (this page) and cut a hole in the tip. (The larger you cut the hole, the wider the outline.) Hold the pastry cone at a 45-degree angle to the cookie surface and apply consistent, gentle pressure while moving the cone in the direction you want the icing to go. Do not drag the tip of the cone in the

How to Make and Use a Parchment Pastry Cone

I use this humble DIY cone to guide icing when flooding cookies, as a funnel when sanding cookie tops, and for many other cooking decorating techniques. Because the hole in the tip can be cut smaller than the smallest metal pastry tip, a parchment cone allows for greater precision than a canvas or plastic pastry bag. What's more, it's easier to clean up—simply toss it when it's empty.

- **To make:** Cut a piece of parchment paper into a perfect square (about 15 x 15 inches) and then cut that square along the diagonal into two triangles. (You'll make one cone from each triangle.)
- Hold the triangle from the two corners on either end of its longest side, with the longest side facing away from you.
- Roll in one corner to the center of the triangle to form a half-cone. (The tip of the half-cone should be at the midpoint of the longest side of the triangle. The open end of the half-cone should be facing toward you.)
- While holding the half-cone in position with one hand, use your other hand to wrap the remaining half of the triangle around the half-cone. (The three corners of the triangle should now be side by side, at the open end of the cone.)

- Close any hole in the tip of the cone by pulling down on one of the triangle corners at the open end of the cone. (It's best that there be no hole at this stage. This way, you can cut the hole as big or as small as you want once the cone is filled with icing.)
- To keep the cone from unraveling, fold down the triangle corners so they lie on the outside of the cone; then cut a notch in this fold and turn the notch down.
- **To use:** Fill the cone half to two-thirds full with Royal Icing. You'll have greater control if the cone isn't overloaded; plus, the icing will be less likely to flow out of the top as you work. Roll down the paper at the top of the cone until it meets the Royal Icing.
- Cut a hole of the desired size in the tip and apply steady pressure at the top of the cone to push the icing through the tip. Do not squeeze from the middle of the cone, or the icing can flow out the top. As you use icing, continue to roll down the top of the cone. (Any empty space in the cone makes it harder to push the icing through the tip.)

Stand-in

While you're getting the hang of making parchment pastry cones, you can always substitute a plastic baggie with a hole snipped in one corner. But because baggies are floppy, don't expect this stand-in to be as easy to grip and control.

icing; rather, hold the tip about ¼ inch above the cookie and allow the icing to fall into place. If the icing breaks as you are drawing, you are likely moving too fast. If the icing falls back onto itself rather than in a straight line, you are probably moving the cone too slowly.

4. Flooding (aka running in sugar, pictured p. 97) describes the process of "flooding" a relatively loose Royal Icing into an area defined by a preexisting outline. I rarely flood the entire cookie surface (in lieu of top-coating), as it's often quicker to top-coat first and then outline. However, if I'm having trouble keeping the top coat from flowing off a very small cookie, or if I want to contain icing in a tight angular area, I will outline first to create a "dam" and then flood with a looser icing.

    To flood, fill a parchment pastry cone with Royal Icing thinned to top-coating consistency (p. 152) and cut a hole in the tip. Guide the icing around the interior of the outline until the area is

completely filled. *Note:* If your outline color is different than your flooding color, be sure to let the outline dry completely before flooding. Otherwise, the colors may bleed.

5. Beadwork (pictured, p. 97). To make a bead, fill a parchment pastry cone with Royal Icing thinned to beadwork consistency (p. 152) and cut a hole of the desired size in the tip. Hold the pastry cone at a 90-degree angle to the cookie with the tip nearly on the cookie surface. Apply gentle pressure until the dot reaches the desired size; then stop applying pressure and quickly pull the cone straight up. To create a beaded border, pipe a series of dots along the edge of the cookie top coat.

6. Dusting (pictured, p. 130) refers to the application of dry luster dust (an edible iridescent powder) to a hard, dry top coat or to an

un-iced cookie. Use a small, dry paintbrush that is properly sized for your task. For a very confined area, the smaller the brush, the better. Luster dust is available in a rainbow of colors at most cake decorating supply stores or online (p. 156).

7. Painting (pictured, p. 130) is an extension of dusting that uses a "paint" made from luster dust mixed with clear extract. The paint is brushed onto a dry top coat or bare cookie. After the alcohol in the extract evaporates, a dry, shiny residue is left behind.

    Start with roughly equal proportions of dust to extract and test the paint on the back of a cookie. For a more translucent finish, add more extract; for a heavier finish, add more dust. As the paint sits, the alcohol will evaporate and the paint will get thicker, so be prepared to make consistency adjustments throughout the painting process.

    Allow any leftover paint to dry in the container in which it was mixed. Once dry, the powder can be returned to its original container and saved for future use. *Note:* Cookie paint can also be made by extending soft gel food coloring with extract; however, this paint will not be iridescent.

8. Sanding (aka flocking, pictured p. 32) is the mass-application of small decorations, such as sanding sugar, nonpareils, or dragées (also called sugar beads), to cookies. (*Note:* 1 mm dragées are easier on the teeth than standard 3 mm dragées and are therefore better for sanding purposes.) For sources of these decorations, see page 156.

    To avoid messy cleanup, sand over a bowl. Either sprinkle the decorations by hand or funnel them through a parchment pastry cone onto wet Royal Icing. You can sand an entire cookie by first coating it with Royal Icing, or you can sand a smaller area or even a thin line. But remember, if you do not want to sand a certain part of the cookie, the icing in that area must be completely dry. After applying the decorations, gently shake off any excess into the bowl and funnel back into the original storage container for re-use.

9. Stenciling (pictured, p. 66). Either bare or top-coated cookies may be stenciled, but if you choose the latter, make sure the top coats have dried to the point of being quite hard (usually overnight).

    Mix Royal Icing to stenciling consistency (p. 152) and tint it to contrast the color of your top coats (or bare cookies). Choose a stencil that lies very flat across the cookie and whose pattern fits the cookie top with some room to spare. (See page 156 for stencil sources.) If your stencil is too large, it can lift up at the cookie edges, allowing icing to sneak underneath into areas where it shouldn't be.

    With one hand, hold the stencil firmly against the cookie top.

With the other hand, grab a small offset spatula and spread a thin layer of icing over the openings in the stencil. Do not move the stencil while applying the icing, or the resulting pattern will be blurred. Lift the stencil slowly and steadily off the cookie; then wipe any icing off the bottom of the stencil before proceeding to the next cookie. For the sharpest patterns, wash and thoroughly dry the stencil after every 2 or 3 icing applications.

10. Appliqué work (pictured pp. 83, 112, and 113) describes the arrangement of relatively large elements—i.e., dragées, pre-formed fondant decorations (p. 155), sugarcoated edible flowers, or other decorated cookies—on top-coated or un-iced cookies. Fondant and standard 3 mm dragées can be found in most cake decorating supply stores. Sugarcoated flowers and larger (4 to 7 mm) dragées are especially striking; however, they are easiest to find online (p. 156).

    Make sure cookie top coats are dry before applying any items to them. Pipe a small amount of icing where you want to place the item(s); then set the item(s) on top. Let the icing dry about ½ hour before moving the cookies. (For precise placement of small items, such as 3 mm dragées, use a clean pair of tweezers.)

11. Papering (pictured, pp. 48 and 50) is the application of wafer paper—thin, translucent sheets of dehydrated potato starch, water, and vegetable oil—to cookie tops. Wafer paper comes both plain and preprinted with food-safe dyes in many patterns. You can even put your own designs on plain paper using markers filled with food coloring, or rubber stamps or paintbrushes dipped in the same. For sources of wafer paper and food-safe markers, see page 156.

    Wafer paper will only adhere to cookies that have been top-coated with Royal Icing or covered with a layer of fondant. Let top coats and fondant coverings dry thoroughly, ideally overnight, before applying any paper.

    To completely cover a cookie with wafer paper, lightly trace the cookie shape onto the paper using the cookie cutter (used to make the cookie) as your guide. Cut out the shape and trim the edges to remove all tracing marks. Use a small sponge brush to thinly coat the back of the paper with light corn syrup; then turn the paper over and gently press it onto the cookie top. Smooth any bubbles by running your fingers over the paper and press down all edges, as they otherwise may lift.

    Let paper-covered cookies dry several hours before adding Royal Icing borders or other icing details. (If you add icing borders when the paper is still moist, the edges are more likely to lift.)

Fun with Fondant

- Fondant is a sugar dough that can be rolled and shaped into ribbons and other 3-D garnishes for cookies and cakes. When left to air-dry, it will harden and hold its shape. (It will also become brittle and fragile, so handle dried pieces carefully.) Fondant is available in most cake decorating supply stores and online. See page 156 for sources.

- Fondant is pure white, but it can be tinted to any shade simply by kneading in soft gel food coloring of your choice.

- **To make ribbons, such as the hat bands on Shortbread Easter Bonnets (p. 42 and below):** Roll fondant into thin sheets with a pasta machine or rolling pin and cut out ribbons of the desired width and length using a ruler as your guide. Glue them into place on the cookies with Royal Icing while the fondant is still pliable.

- **For daisies and leaves, such as those on Shortbread Easter Bonnets:** Roll fondant into thin sheets with a pasta machine or rolling pin, and cut out the desired shapes with cookie cutters. If you want the fondant pieces to conform to the cookies, secure them while the dough is still pliable. Otherwise, shape as you wish and let the pieces air-dry before attaching them.

- **For bows, such as those on the gingerbread Easter baskets (p. 32):** Shape small segments of fondant ribbon into loops and stick the ends together with a bit of water to form bows. Cover the ends of the loops by wrapping another ribbon around the center of each bow. Allow the bows to air-dry until they hold their shape; then secure to gingerbread baskets or other cookies with thick Royal Icing. (Drying time varies with bow size.)

- **For cords, such as the handles on the gingerbread Easter baskets:** Roll fondant into two ropes of the desired diameter and length for your project. (For the handles on the baskets, I used two 26- to 30-inch ropes, each about ¼ inch in diameter.) Twist the two ropes together on your work surface to form a cord and trim the ends to neaten. Avoid lifting long cords while twisting, as they can stretch and misshape. To make a handle from the cord, shape it into an arc on a cookie sheet, and air-dry until it can be lifted without bending or breaking. (Very large handles, such as the ones on the baskets, may need to dry as long as a couple of weeks, so plan ahead.)

- **For vines, such as those on Great Pumpkin Cookies (p. 120 and below):** Roll small portions of fondant into thin ropes that taper to a point at one end. Wrap each rope around a thin (¼-inch-diameter or less) dowel rod and dry a few minutes, or until the vine holds its shape when slipped off the rod. Apply the vines to the cookies while still pliable or allow them to dry completely for easier handling.

Many of the cookie tools and decorations listed here can be found in kitchenware and cake decorating supply stores. If your local suppliers don't bear fruit, my favorite online sources, below, are a sure bet.

	Cookie cutters	Cotton candy	Decorative do-dads, i.e., nonpareils, dragées, and sanding sugar	Dishers (aka cookie scoops)	Fondant	Food-safe markers	Gumballs	Lavender flowers	Luster dust	Papier-mâché boxes, pots, and baskets	Royal icing flowers and decorations	Soft gel food coloring	Specialty extracts	Specialty oils and other flavorings	Springerle molds and rolling pins	Stencils	Sugarcoated edible flowers	Wafer paper
Boyajian boyajianinc.com 781-828-9966 / 800-965-0665														X (wide range, including citrus oils)				
Craft Supplies Online craft-supplies-online.com 800-999-9513										X (wide range of boxes and baskets)								
D. Blümchen & Company blumchen.com 866-653-9627										X (boxes only, including nested egg boxes)								
Designer Stencils designerstencils.com 302-475-7300 / 800-822-7836																X (custom options available)		
Fancy Flours fancyflours.com 406-587-0118	X		X		X	X			X		X	X		X		X	X	X (wide range)
gumballs.com 888-860-6506							X											
H. O. Foose Tinsmithing Co. foosecookiecutters.com 610-944-1960	X (wide range, plus DIY cookie cutter–making kits)																	
House on the Hill, Inc. houseonthehill.net 630-279-4455 / 877-279-4455	X			X		X			X			X	X	X (citrus and cinnamon oils, rosewater)	X (wide range of both molds and pins)			
Kitchen Collectables kitchengifts.com 888-593-2436	X (custom options available)		X			X			X			X		X (natural cinnamon flavoring)				
Nature's Flavors naturesflavors.com 714-744-3700													X (wide range of organic options, including cinnamon and pistachio)	X (wide range of organic options, including hazelnut, cinnamon, and citrus flavoring)				

	Cookie cutters	Cotton candy	Decorative do-dads, i.e., nonpareils, dragées, and sanding sugar	Dishers (aka cookie scoops)	Fondant	Food-safe markers	Gumballs	Lavender flowers	Luster dust	Papier-mâché boxes, pots, and baskets	Royal icing flowers and decorations	Soft gel food coloring	Specialty extracts	Specialty oils and other flavorings	Springerle molds and rolling pins	Stencils	Sugarcoated edible flowers	Wafer paper
Off the Beaten Path cookiecutter.com 816-415-8827 / 866-756-6543	X (custom options available)		X			X			X									
OK Manufacturing, LLC gumballs.net 801-974-9116 / 800-748-5480							X											
Papa John's Peanuts, Inc. papajohnspeanuts.biz 866-757-6887		X																
Penzeys Spices penzeys.com 800-741-7787								X										
Silver Cloud Estates silvercloudestates.com 410-484-4526													X (wide range, including cinnamon and hazelnut)	X (wide range, including natural pistachio flavoring)				
Stencil Planet stencilplanet.com 908-771-8967 / 877-836-2457																X (custom options available)		
Surfas Restaurant and Supply surfasonline.com 310-559-4770 / 866-799-4770			X	X				X	X				X (wide range, including coffee)	X (rosewater)				
Sweet Celebrations sweetc.com 800-328-6722	X		X		X	X			X		X	X	X	X		X		X (plain paper only)
Sweetfields sweetfields.com 760-522-3422 / 877-987-9338																	X	
The Bernod Group bernod.com 661-295-9833		X																
The Cookie Cutter Shop thecookiecuttershop.com 360-652-3295	X (wide range)																	
The Spice House thespicehouse.com 312-274-0378								X					X (coffee)	X (rosewater)				
Vanilla, Saffron Imports saffron.com 415-648-8990													X (wide range, including pistachio)					

INDEX

Metric Conversion Chart

Volume Measurements		Weight Measurements		Temperature Conversion	
U.S.	Metric	U.S.	Metric	Fahrenheit	Celsius
1 teaspoon	5 ml	½ ounce	15 g	250	120
1 tablespoon	15 ml	1 ounce	30 g	300	150
¼ cup	60 ml	3 ounces	90 g	325	160
⅓ cup	75 ml	4 ounces	115 g	350	180
½ cup	125 ml	8 ounces	225 g	375	190
⅔ cup	150 ml	12 ounces	350 g	400	200
¾ cup	175 ml	1 pound	450 g	425	220
1 cup	250 ml	2¼ pounds	1 kg	450	230

Equivalents are not exact; figures have been rounded up or down for easier measuring.

By weight, a cup is not the same for all ingredients. Volume equivalents, above, apply to liquids only. Dry ingredients should be weighed and scaled using the following approximate equivalents: all-purpose flour, spooned and leveled (approximately 4½ ounces, 130 g), granulated sugar (approximately 7 ounces, 200 g), packed light brown sugar (approximately 7⅔ ounces, 215 g).